Uganda

Renee Browning

Contents

Articles

References

Overview of Uganda

Uganda

Republic of Uganda Jamhuri ya Uganda	
Motto: "For God and My Country"	
Anthem: Oh Uganda, Land of Beauty	
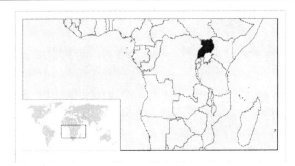	
Capital (and largest city)	Kampala
Official language(s)	English
Vernacular languages	Luganda, Luo, Runyankore, Ateso, Lumasaba, Lusoga, Lunyole, Samia
Demonym	Ugandan
Government	Democratic Republic
- President	Yoweri Museveni
- Vice President	Gilbert Bukenya
- Prime Minister	Apolo Nsibambi
Independence	from the United Kingdom
- Republic	9 October 1962

Area		
-	Total	236,040 km^2 (81st) 91,136 sq mi
-	Water (%)	15.39
Population		
-	2009 estimate	32,369,558 (37th)
-	2002 census	24,227,297
-	Density	137.1/km^2 (80th) 355.2/sq mi
GDP (PPP)	2009 estimate	
-	Total	$39.686 billion
-	Per capita	$1,195
GDP (nominal)	2009 estimate	
-	Total	$15.736 billion
-	Per capita	$474
Gini (1998)	43 (medium)	
HDI (2008)	▲ 0.514 (medium) (157th)	
Currency	Ugandan shilling (UGX)	
Time zone	EAT (UTC+3)	
-	Summer (DST)	*not observed* (UTC+3)
Drives on the	left	
ISO 3166 code	UG	
Internet TLD	.ug	
Calling code	+256[1]	

[1] 006 from Kenya and Tanzania.

Geographical coordinates: 1°17′N 32°23′E

The **Republic of Uganda** (pronounced /juːˈɡændə/ *yew-GAN-də* or /juːˈɡɑːndə/ *yew-GAHN-də*) is a landlocked country in East Africa. It is bordered on the east by Kenya, on the north by Sudan, on the west by the Democratic Republic of the Congo, on the southwest by Rwanda, and on the south by Tanzania. The southern part of the country includes a substantial portion of Lake Victoria, which is also bordered by Kenya and Tanzania.

Uganda takes its name from the Buganda kingdom, which encompassed a portion of the south of the country including the capital Kampala.

The people of Uganda were hunter-gatherers until 1,700 to 2,300 years ago, when Bantu-speaking populations migrated to the southern parts of the country. Uganda gained independence from Britain in 1962.

The official languages are English and Swahili, although multiple other languages are spoken in the country.

It is a member of the African Union, the Commonwealth of Nations, Organisation of the Islamic Conference and East African Community.

History

Main article: History of Uganda

The people of Uganda were hunter-gatherers until 1,700 to 2,300 years ago. Bantu-speaking populations, who were probably from central and western Africa, migrated to the southern parts of the country. These groups brought and developed ironworking skills and new ideas of social and political organization. The Empire of Kitara in the fourteenth and fifteenth centuries represents the earliest forms of formal organization, followed by the kingdom of Bunyoro-Kitara, and in later centuries, Buganda and Ankole.

Nilotic people including Luo and Ateker entered the area from the north, probably beginning about A.D. 120. They were cattle herders and subsistence farmers who settled mainly the northern and eastern parts of the country. Some Luo invaded the area of Bunyoro and assimilated with the Bantu there, establishing the Babiito dynasty of the current *Omukama* (ruler) of Bunyoro-Kitara. Luo migration continued until the 16th century, with some Luo settling amid Bantu people in Eastern Uganda, with others proceeding to the western shores of Lake Victoria in Kenya and Tanzania. The Ateker (Karimojong and Iteso) settled in the northeastern and eastern parts of the country, and some fused with the Luo in the area north of Lake Kyoga.

Arab traders moved inland from the Indian Ocean coast of East Africa in the 1830s. They were followed in the 1860s by British explorers searching for the source of the Nile. Protestant missionaries entered the country in 1877, followed by Catholic missionaries in 1879. The United Kingdom placed the area under the charter of the British East Africa Company in 1888, and ruled it as a protectorate from 1894.

20th century

As several other territories and chiefdoms were integrated, the final protectorate called Uganda took shape in 1914. From 1900 to 1920, a sleeping sickness epidemic killed more than 250,000 people, about two-thirds of the population in the affected lake-shore areas.

Uganda gained independence from Britain in 1962, maintaining its Commonwealth membership. The first post-independence election, held in 1962, was won by an alliance between the Uganda People's Congress (UPC) and Kabaka Yekka (KY). UPC and KY formed the first post-independence government with Milton Obote as executive Prime Minister, the Buganda Kabaka (King) Edward Muteesa II holding the largely ceremonial position of President and William Wilberforce Nadiope, the Kyabazinga (paramount chief) of Busoga, as Vice President.[citation needed]

In 1966, following a power struggle between the Obote-led government and King Muteesa, the UPC-dominated Parliament changed the constitution and removed the ceremonial president and vice president. In 1967, a new constitution proclaimed Uganda a republic and abolished the traditional kingdoms. Without first calling elections, Obote was declared the executive President.

Obote was deposed from office in 1971 when Idi Amin seized power. Amin ruled the country with the military for the next eight years. Amin's rule cost an estimated 300,000 Ugandans' lives. He forcibly removed the entrepreneurial Indian minority from Uganda. The Ugandan economy was devastated.

Amin's reign was ended after the Uganda-Tanzania War in 1979 in which Tanzanian forces aided by Ugandan exiles invaded Uganda. This led to the return of Obote, who was deposed once more in 1985 by General Tito Okello. Okello ruled for six months until he was deposed after the so called "bush war" by the National Resistance Army (NRA) operating under the leadership of the current president, Yoweri Museveni, and various rebel groups, including the Federal Democratic Movement of Andrew Kayiira, and another belonging to John Nkwaanga.

Museveni has been in power since 1986. In the mid to late 1990s, he was lauded by the West as part of a new generation of African leaders. His presidency has included involvement in the civil war in the Democratic Republic of Congo (DRC) and other conflicts in the Great Lakes region, as well as the civil war against the Lord's Resistance Army, which has been guilty of numerous crimes against humanity including child slavery and mass murder. Conflict in northern Uganda has killed thousands and displaced millions. In 2007, Uganda deployed soldiers to the African Union peacekeeping mission in Somalia.[citation needed]

Government

Yoweri Museveni, President of Uganda.

Main article: Politics of Uganda

The President of Uganda, currently Yoweri kaguta Museveni, is both head of state and head of government. The president appoints a Vice President, currently Gilbert Bukenya and a prime minister, currently Apolo Nsibambi, who aid him in governing. The parliament is formed by the National Assembly, which has 332 members. 104 of these members are nominated by interest groups, including women and the army. The remaining members are elected for four year terms during general elections.

Political parties were restricted in their activities from 1986 in a measure ostensibly designed to reduce sectarian violence. In the non-party "Movement" system instituted by Museveni, political parties continued to exist, but they could only operate a headquarters office. They could not open branches, hold rallies, or field candidates directly (although electoral candidates could belong to political parties). A constitutional referendum canceled this nineteen-year ban on multi-party politics in July 2005. Additionally, the time limit for president was changed in the constitution from the two-term limit in order to enable the current president to continue in active politics.

The presidential elections were held in February, 2006. Yoweri Museveni ran against several candidates, the most prominent of whom was exiled Dr. Kizza Besigye.

Geography

Main article: Geography of Uganda

The country is located on the East African plateau, averaging about 1100 metres (3609 ft) above sea level, and this slopes very steadily downwards to the Sudanese Plain to the north. However, much of the south is poorly drained, while the centre is dominated by Lake Kyoga, which is also surrounded by extensive marshy areas. Uganda lies almost completely within the Nile basin. The Victoria Nile drains from the lake into Lake Kyoga and thence into Lake Albert on the Congolese border. It then runs northwards into Sudan. One small area on the eastern edge of Uganda is drained by the Turkwel river, part of the internal drainage basin of Lake Turkana.

Map of Uganda

Lake Kyoga serves as a rough boundary between Bantu speakers in the south and Nilotic and Central Sudanic language speakers in the north. Despite the division between north and south in political affairs, this linguistic boundary actually runs roughly from northwest to southeast, near the course of the Nile. However, many Ugandans live among people who speak different languages, especially in rural areas. Some sources describe regional variation in terms of physical characteristics, clothing, bodily adornment, and mannerisms, but others claim that those differences are disappearing.

Although generally equatorial, the climate is not uniform as the altitude modifies the climate. Southern Uganda is wetter with rain generally spread throughout the year. At Entebbe on the northern shore of Lake Victoria, most rain falls from March to June and the November/December period. Further to the north a dry season gradually emerges; at Gulu about 120 km from the Sudanese border, November to February is much drier than the rest of the year.

The northeastern Karamoja region has the driest climate and is prone to droughts in some years. Rwenzori in the southwest on the border with Congo (DRC) receives heavy rain all year round. The south of the country is heavily influenced by one of the world's biggest lakes, Lake Victoria, which contains many islands. It prevents temperatures from varying significantly and increases cloudiness and rainfall. Most important cities are located in the south, near Lake Victoria, including the capital Kampala and the nearby city of Entebbe.

Although landlocked, Uganda contains many large lakes, besides Lake Victoria and Lake Kyoga, there are Lake Albert, Lake Edward and the smaller Lake George.

Districts, counties, and kingdoms

Main articles: Districts of Uganda, Counties of Uganda, and Sub-counties of Uganda

See also: List of cities and towns in Uganda

Uganda is divided into 80 districts, spread across four administrative regions: Northern, Eastern, Central (Kingdom of Buganda) and Western. The districts are subdivided into counties. A number of districts have been added in the past few years, and eight others were added on July 1, 2006. Most districts are named after their main commercial and administrative towns. Each district is divided into sub-districts, counties, sub-counties, parishes and villages.

Parallel with the state administration, six traditional Bantu kingdoms have remained, enjoying some degrees of mainly cultural autonomy. The kingdoms are Toro, Ankole, Busoga, Bunyoro, Buganda and Rwenzururu.

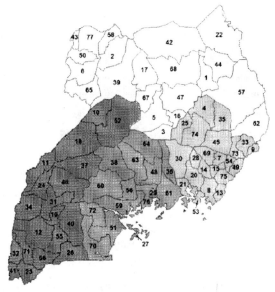

Districts of Uganda

Economy

Main articles: Economy of Uganda and Energy in Uganda

For decades, Uganda's economy suffered from devastating economic policies and instability, leaving Uganda as one of the world's poorest countries. The country has commenced economic reforms and growth has been robust. In 2008, Uganda recorded 7% growth despite the global downturn and regional instability.

Uganda has substantial natural resources, including fertile soils, regular rainfall, and sizable mineral deposits of copper and cobalt.

Downtown Kampala

The country has largely untapped reserves of both crude oil and natural gas. While agriculture used to account for 56% of the economy in 1986, with coffee as its main export, it has now been surpassed by the Services sector, which accounted for 52% of percent GDP in 2007. In the 1950s the British Colonial regime encouraged some 500,000 subsistence farmers to join co-operatives. Since 1986, the government (with the support of foreign countries and international agencies) has acted to rehabilitate an economy devastated during the regime of Idi Amin and subsequent civil war. Inflation ran at 240% in 1987 and 42% in June 1992, and was 5.1% in 2003.

Between 1990 and 2001, the economy grew because of continued investment in the rehabilitation of infrastructure, improved incentives for production and exports, reduced inflation, gradually improved domestic security, and the return of exiled Indian-Ugandan entrepreneurs between 1990 and 2001. [*citation needed*] Ongoing Ugandan involvement in the war in the Democratic Republic of the Congo, corruption within the government, and slippage in the government's determination to press reforms raise doubts about the continuation of strong growth.

In 2000, Uganda was included in the Heavily Indebted Poor Countries (HIPC) debt relief initiative worth $1.3 billion and Paris Club debt relief worth $145 million. These amounts combined with the original HIPC debt relief added up to about $2 billion.But in 2006 the Ugandan Government successfully paid all their debts to the Paris Club, which meant that it was no longer in the(HIPC)list. Growth for 2001–2002 was solid despite continued decline in the price of coffee, Uganda's principal export. According to IMF statistics, in 2004 Uganda's GDP per capita reached $300, a much higher level than in the 1980s but still at half the Sub-Saharan African average income of $600 per year. Total GDP crossed the 8 billion dollar mark in the same year.

Economic growth has not always led to poverty reduction. Despite an average annual growth of 2.5% between 2000 and 2003, poverty levels increased by 3.8% during that time. This has highlighted the importance of avoiding jobless growth and is part of the rising awareness in development circles of the need for equitable growth not just in Uganda, but across the developing world.

With the Uganda securities exchanges established in 1996, several equities have been listed. The Government has used the stock market as an avenue for privatisation. All Government treasury issues are listed on the securities exchange. The Capital Markets Authority has licensed 18 brokers, asset managers and investment advisors including names like African Alliance, AIG Investments, Renaissance Capital and SIMMS. As one of the ways of increasing formal domestic savings, Pension sector reform is the centre of attention (2007).

Uganda depends on Kenya for access to international markets. Uganda is part of the East African Community and a potential member of the planned East African Federation.

Demographics

Main article: Demographics of Uganda

See also: Languages of Uganda and Religion in Uganda

Uganda is home to many different ethnic groups, none of whom forms a majority of the population. Around forty different languages are regularly and currently in use in the country. English became the official language of Uganda after independence. Ugandan English has a local flavour.

The most widely spoken local language in Uganda is Luganda, spoken predominantly by the Baganda people in the urban concentrations of Kampala, the capital city, and in towns and localities in the Buganda region of Uganda which encompasses Kampala. The Lusoga and Runyankore languages follow, spoken predominantly in the southeastern and southwestern parts of Uganda respectively.

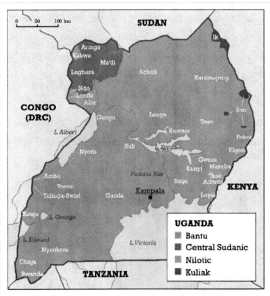

Ethnolinguistic map of Uganda.

Swahili, a widely used language throughout eastern and central east Africa, was approved as the country's second official national language in 2005, though this is somewhat politically sensitive. Though the language has not been favoured by the Bantu-speaking populations of the south and southwest of the country, it is an important *lingua franca* in the northern regions. It is also widely used in the police and military forces, which may be a historical result of the disproportionate recruitment of northerners into the security forces during the colonial period. The status of Swahili has thus alternated with the political group in power. For example, Amin, who came from the northwest, declared Swahili to be the national language.

Uganda's population has grown from 4.8 million people in 1950 to 24.3 million in 2002. The current estimated population of Uganda is 32.4 million. Uganda has a very young population, with a median age of 15 years.

Religion

Main article: Religion in Uganda

Religion in Uganda	
religion	percent
Roman Catholicism	42%
Protestantism	42%
Islam	12%
Other or None	4%

According to the census of 2002, Christians made up about 84% of Uganda's population. The Roman Catholic Church has the largest number of adherents (41.9%), followed by the Anglican Church of Uganda (35.9%). The next most reported religion of Uganda is Islam, with Muslims representing 12% of the population.

Ugandan woman

The census lists only 1% of Uganda's population as following traditional religions, and 0.7% are classified as 'other non-Christians,' including adherents of sects. In addition to a small community of Jewish expatriates centered in Kampala, Uganda is home to the Abayudaya, a native Jewish community dating from the early 1900s. One of the world's seven Bahá'í Houses of Worship is located on the outskirts of Kampala. See also Bahá'í Faith in Uganda.

According to the *World Refugee Survey 2008*, published by the U.S. Committee for Refugees and Immigrants, Uganda hosted a population of refugees and asylum seekers numbering 235,800 in 2007. The majority of this population came from Sudan (162,100 persons), but also included refugees and asylum seekers from the Democratic Republic of the Congo (41,800), Rwanda (21,200), Somalia (5,700) and Burundi (3,100).

Of the Christian population, the Roman Catholic Church has the largest number of followers, followed by the Anglican Church, while Evangelical and Pentecostal churches claim the rest. The Muslim population is primarily Sunni and in minority, the Ahmadiyya Muslim Community. Traditional indigenous beliefs are practiced in some rural areas and are sometimes blended with or practiced alongside Christianity or Islam. Indian nationals are the most significant immigrant population; members of this community are primarily Ismaili (Shi'a Muslim followers of the Aga Khan) or Hindu. More than 30 years ago, there were about 80,000 Indians in Uganda. Today there are about 15,000. The northern and West Nile regions are predominantly Catholic, while Iganga District in eastern Uganda has the highest percentage of Muslims. The rest of the country has a mix of religious affiliations.

Health

Main articles: Health in Uganda and HIV/AIDS in Uganda

Uganda has been among the rare HIV success stories, one of the reasons being openness. It has been reported that 95% of all Ugandans ages 15–49 claim to practice monogamy. This is supported by the findings of a 2006 study that modern contraceptive use in Uganda is low.

Infant mortality rate was at 79 per 1,000 in 2005. Life expectancy was at 50.2 for females, and 49.1 for males in 2005. There were 8 physicians per 100,000 persons in the early 2000s.

Uganda's elimination of user fees at state health facilities in 2001 has resulted in an 80% increase in visits; over half of this increase is from the poorest 20% of the population. This policy has been cited as a key factor in helping Uganda achieve its Millennium Development Goals and as an example of the importance of equity in achieving those goals.

Culture and sport

Main articles: Culture of Uganda, Music of Uganda, List of African writers (by country)#Uganda, and List of Ugandans

Owing to the large number of communities, culture within Uganda is diverse. Many Asians (mostly from India) who were expelled during the regime of Amin have returned to Uganda.[citation needed]

Young boys playing football in Arua District

Cricket has experienced rapid growth although football is the most popular sport in Uganda. Recently in the Quadrangular Tournament in Kenya, Uganda came in as the underdogs and went on to register a historic win against archrivals Kenya. Uganda also won the World Cricket League (WCL) Division 3 and came in fourth place in the WCL Division 2. In February 2009, Uganda finished as runner-up in the WCL Division 3 competition held in Argentina, thus gaining a place in the World Cup Qualifier held in South Africa in April 2009. In 2007 the Ugandan Rugby Union team were victorious in the 2007 Africa Cup, beating Madagascar in the final.

Rallying is also a popular sport in Uganda with the country having successfully staged a round of the African Rally Championship (ARC), Pearl of Africa Rally since 1996 when it was a candidate event. The country has gone on to produce African rally champions such as Charles Muhangi who won the

1999 ARC crown. Other notable Ugandans on the African rally scene include the late Riyaz Kurji who was killed in an fatal accident while leading the 2009 edition, Emma Katto, Karim Hirji, Chipper Adams and Charles Lubega. Ugandans have also featured prominently in the Safari Rally.

Ugandans have since the early twenties enjoyed the fast-paced sport of hockey. It was originally played by the Asians, but now it is widely played by people from other racial backgrounds. Hockey is the only Ugandan field sport to date to have qualified for and represented the country at the Olympics; this was at the Munich games in 1972. It is also believed in Ugandan hockey circles that Uganda's first and only Olympic gold medal may have been realized in part by the cheers from the representative hockey team that urged John Akii-Bua forward.[citation needed]

Education

Main article: Education in Uganda

Illiteracy is common in Uganda, particularly among females. Public spending on education was at 5.2 % of the 2002–2005 GDP. Much public education in primary and secondary schools focus upon repetition and memorization. There are also state exams that must be taken at every level of education. Uganda has both private and public universities. The largest university in Uganda is Makerere University located outside of Kampala.

Human rights

Main article: Human rights in Uganda

Respect for human rights in Uganda has been advanced significantly since the mid-1980s. There are, however, numerous areas which continue to attract concern.

Conflict in the northern parts of the country continues to generate reports of abuses by both the rebel Lord's Resistance Army and the Ugandan army. A UN official accused the LRA in February 2009 of "appalling brutality" in the Democratic Republic of Congo. The number of internally displaced persons is estimated at 1.4 million. Torture continues to be a widespread practice amongst security organizations. Attacks on political freedom in the country, including the arrest and beating of opposition Members of Parliament, has led to international criticism, culminating in May 2005 in a decision by the British government to withhold part of its aid to the country. The arrest of the main opposition leader Kizza Besigye and the besiegement of the High Court during a hearing of Besigye's case by a heavily armed security forces — before the February 2006 elections — led to condemnation.

Recently, grassroots organizations have been attempting to raise awareness about the children who were kidnapped by the Lord's Resistance Army to work as soldiers or be used as wives. Thousands of children as young as eight were captured and forced to kill. The documentary film *Invisible Children* illustrates the terrible lives of the children, known as night commuters, who still to this day leave their villages and walk many miles each night to avoid abduction.

The U.S. Committee for Refugees and Immigrants reported several violations of refugee rights in 2007, including forcible deportations by the Ugandan government and violence directed against refugees.

See also

Main articles: Outline of Uganda and Index of Uganda-related articles

- List of schools in Uganda
- The Uganda Scouts Association
- List of national parks of Uganda
- Kisiizi
- *War/Dance*
- Cabinet of Uganda
- Uganda AIDS Orphan Children Foundation

External links

Uganda travel guide from Wikitravel

- Chief of State and Cabinet Members [1]
- Uganda [2] entry at *The World Factbook*
- Uganda [3] from *UCB Libraries GovPubs*
- Uganda [4] at the Open Directory Project
- Wikimedia Atlas of Uganda
- Humanitarian news and analysis from IRIN – Uganda [5]
- Humanitarian information coverage on ReliefWeb [6]
- Country Profile [7] from BBC News
- Uganda Tourist Board [8]
- Uganda travel guide from Wikitravel
- Uganda Humanist Schools Trust [9]
- UG Pulse [10] with daily photos of Uganda
- Necklaces made in Uganda [11]
- Radio France International – dossier on Uganda and Lord's Resistance Army [12]

ace:Uganda mhr:Уганда pnb:اۏگنڈا

History

History of Uganda

History of Uganda
This article is part of **a series**
Chronology
Early history (before 1894)
British rule (1894–1962)
Early independence (1962–71)
Under Idi Amin (1971–1979)
Recent history (1979–present)
Special themes
Expulsion of Asians
History of Buganda
LRA insurgency
Military history of Uganda
Ugandan Bush War
Uganda–Tanzania War
Uganda Portal

The **history of Uganda** comprises the history of the territory of present-day Uganda in East Africa and the peoples inhabating the region.

Uganda before 1900

Main article: Uganda before 1900

The earliest human inhabitants in a contemporary Uganda were hunter-gathers. Remnants of these people are today to be found among the pygmies in western Uganda. Between approximately 2500 to 1500 years ago, Bantu speaking populations from central and western Africa migrated and occupied most of the southern parts of the country. This culture was part of the Urewe, or early eastern Bantu cultural complex. The migrants brought with them agriculture, ironworking skills and new ideas of social and political organization, that by the fifteenth or sixteenth century resulted in the development of centralized kingdoms, including the kingdoms of Buganda, Bunyoro-Kitara and Ankole.

Nilotic people, including Luo and Ateker entered the area from the north probably beginning about AD 1000. They were cattle herders and subsistence farmers who settled mainly the northern and eastern parts of the country. Some Luo invaded the area of Bunyoro and assimilated with the Bantu there, establishing the Babiito dynasty of the current *Omukama* (ruler) of Bunyoro-Kitara in the mid second millennium AD. Luo migration proceeded until the 16th century, with some Luo settling amid Bantu people in Eastern Uganda, and proceeding to the western shores of Lake Victoria in Kenya and Tanzania. The Ateker (Karimojong and Teso peoples) settled in the north-eastern and eastern parts of the country, and some fused with the Luo in the area north of lake Kyoga.

When Arab traders and slavers moved inland from their enclaves along the Indian Ocean coast of East Africa and reached the interior of Uganda in the 1830s, they found several kingdoms with well-developed political institutions. These traders and slavers were followed in the 1860s by British explorers and abolitionists searching for the source of the Nile River and to end slavery. Protestant missionaries entered the country in 1877, followed by Catholic missionaries in 1879.

Colonial Uganda

Main article: Uganda Protectorate

In 1888, control of the emerging British "sphere of interest" in East Africa was assigned by royal charter to William Mackinnon's Imperial British East Africa Company, an arrangement strengthened in 1890 by an Anglo-German agreement confirming British dominance over Kenya and Uganda. The high cost of occupying the territory caused the company to withdraw in 1893, and its administrative functions were taken over by a British commissioner. In 1894, the Kingdom of Uganda was placed under a formal British protectorate.

Early independent Uganda

Main article: Early independent Uganda

Britain granted independence to Uganda in 1962, and the first elections were held on 1 March 1961. Benedicto Kiwanuka of the Democratic Party became the first Chief Minister. Uganda became a republic the following year, maintaining its Commonwealth membership.

In succeeding years, supporters of a centralized state vied with those in favor of a loose federation and a strong role for tribally-based local kingdoms. Political maneuvering climaxed in February 1966, when Prime Minister Milton Obote suspended the constitution and assumed all government powers, removing the positions of president and vice president. In September 1967, a new constitution proclaimed Uganda a republic, gave the president even greater powers, and abolished the traditional kingdoms.

Uganda under Amin

Main article: Uganda under Idi Amin

On 25 January 1971, Obote's government was ousted in a military coup led by armed forces commander Idi Amin Dada. Amin declared himself 'president,' dissolved the parliament, and amended the constitution to give himself absolute power.

Idi Amin's eight-year rule produced economic decline, social disintegration, and massive human rights violations. The Acholi and Langi ethnic groups were particular objects of Amin's political persecution because they had supported Obote and made up a large part of the army. In 1978, the International Commission of Jurists estimated that more than 100,000 Ugandans had been murdered during Amin's reign of terror; some authorities place the figure as high as 300,000—a statistic cited at the end of the 2006 movie The Last King of Scotland, which chronicled part of Amin's dictatorship.

A border altercation involving Ugandan exiles who had a camp close to the Ugandan border of Mutukula resulted into an attack by the Uganda army into Tanzania. In October 1978, Tanzanian armed forces repulsed an incursion of Amin's troops into Tanzanian territory. The Tanzanian army, backed by Ugandan exiles waged a war of liberation against Amin's troops and the Libyan soldiers sent to help him. On 11 April 1979, Kampala was captured, and Amin fled with his remaining forces.

Uganda since 1979

Main article: Uganda since 1979

After Amin's removal, the Uganda National Liberation Front formed an interim government with Yusuf Lule as president and Jeremiah Lucas Opira as the Secretary General of the UNLF. This government adopted a ministerial system of administration and created a quasi-parliamentary organ known as the National Consultative Commission (NCC). The NCC and the Lule cabinet reflected widely differing political views. In June 1979, following a dispute over the extent of presidential powers, the NCC replaced Lule with Godfrey Binaisa. In a continuing dispute over the powers of the interim presidency, Binaisa was removed in May 1980. Thereafter, Uganda was ruled by a military commission chaired by Paulo Muwanga. The December 1980 elections returned the UPC to power under the leadership of President Milton Obote, with Muwanga serving as vice president. Under Obote, the security forces had one of the world's worst human rights records. In their efforts to stamp out an insurgency led by Yoweri Museveni's National Resistance Army (NRA), they laid waste to a substantial section of the country, especially in the Luwero area north of Kampala.

Obote ruled until 27 July 1985, when an army brigade, composed mostly of ethnic Acholi troops and commanded by Lt. Gen. Bazilio Olara-Okello, took Kampala and proclaimed a military government. Obote fled to exile in Zambia. The new regime, headed by former defense force commander Gen. Tito Okello (no relation to Lt. Gen. Olara-Okello), opened negotiations with Museveni's insurgent forces and pledged to improve respect for human rights, end tribal rivalry, and conduct free and fair elections. In the meantime, massive human rights violations continued as the Okello government carried out a brutal counterinsurgency in an attempt to destroy the NRA's support.

Negotiations between the Okello government and the NRA were conducted in Nairobi in the fall of 1985, with Kenyan President Daniel arap Moi seeking a cease-fire and a coalition government in Uganda. Although agreeing in late 1985 to a cease-fire, the NRA continued fighting, and seized Kampala and the country in late January 1986, forcing Okello's forces to flee north into Sudan. Museveni's forces organized a government with Museveni as president.

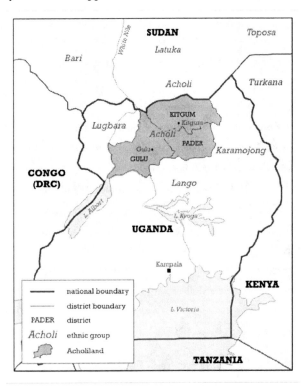

Since assuming power, the government dominated by the political grouping created by Museveni and his followers, the National Resistance Movement (NRM or the "Movement"), has largely put an end to the human rights abuses of earlier governments, initiated substantial political liberalization and general press freedom, and instituted broad economic reforms after consultation with the International Monetary Fund (IMF), World Bank, and donor governments.

In northern areas such as Acholiland, there has been armed resistance against the government since 1986. Acholi based rebel groups include the Uganda People's Democratic Army and the Holy Spirit Movement. Currently, the only remaining rebel group is the Lord's Resistance Army headed by Joseph Kony, which has carried out widespread abduction of children to serve as soldiers or sex slaves.

In 1996, Uganda was a key supporter of the overthrow of Zairean President Mobutu Sese Seko in the First Congo War in favor of rebel leader Laurent-Désiré Kabila. Between 1998 and 2003, the Ugandan army was involved in the Second Congo War in the renamed Democratic Republic of the Congo and the government continues to support rebel groups such as the Movement for the Liberation of Congo and some factions of the Rally for Congolese Democracy.

In August 2005, Parliament voted to change the constitution to lift presidential term limits, allowing Museveni to run for a third term if he wishes to do so. In a referendum in July, 2005, 92.5% supported restoring multiparty politics, thereby scrapping the no-party or "movement" system. Kizza Besigye, Museveni's political rival, returned from exile in October 2005, and was a presidential candidate for the 2006 elections. In the same month, Milton Obote died in South Africa. Museveni won the February 2006 presidential election.

In 2009, the Anti-Homosexuality Bill was proposed and under consideration. It was proposed on 13 October 2009 by Member of Parliament David Bahati and would, if enacted, broaden the criminalization of homosexuality in Uganda, including introducing the death penalty for people who have previous convictions, who are HIV-positive, or who engage in sexual acts with those under 18, introducing extradition for those engaging in same-sex sexual relations outside Uganda, and penalising individuals, companies, media organizations, or NGOs who support LGBT rights.

See also

- Luo History
- Buganda
- History of Africa

References

- ⊚ *This article incorporates public domain material from websites or documents* [1] *of the Library of Congress Country Studies*. - Uganda [2]
- U.S. State Department Background Note: Uganda [3]
- East Africa Living Encyclopedia [4], African Studies Center, University of Pennsylvania
- Origins of Bunyoro-Kitara Kings [5], Bunyoro-Kitara website
- Phyllis Martin and Patrick O'Meara (August 1995), *Africa. 3rd edition*, Indiana University Press

Geography

Geography of Uganda

Uganda is located in Eastern Africa, west of Kenya and east of the Democratic Republic of the Congo. It is in the heart of the Great Lakes region, and is surrounded by three of them, Lake Edward, Lake Albert, and Lake Victoria. While much of its border is lakeshore, Uganda is landlocked with no access to the sea.

Despite being on the equator Uganda is more temperate than the surrounding areas due to its altitude. The country is mostly plateau with a rim of mountains. This has made it more suitable to agriculture and less prone to tropical diseases than other nations in the region. The climate is tropical; generally rainy with two dry seasons (December to February, June to August). It is semiarid East Sudanian savanna in north near Sudan.

Geographic coordinates: 1°00′N 32°00′E

Statistics

Area:
total: 236 040 km²
land: 199 710 km²
water: 36 330 km²

Land boundaries:
total: 2 698 km
border countries: Democratic Republic of the Congo 765 km, Kenya 933 km, Rwanda 169 km, Sudan 435 km, Tanzania 396 km

Elevation extremes:
highest point: Margherita Peak on Mount Stanley 5 110 m

Satellite image of Uganda, generated from raster graphics data supplied by The Map Library

Natural resources: copper, cobalt, hydropower, limestone, salt, arable land

Land use:

arable land: 25%

permanent crops: 9%

permanent pastures: 9%

forests and woodland: 28%

other: 29% (1993 est.)

Irrigated land: 90 km² (1993 est.)

Environment - current issues: draining of wetlands for agricultural use; deforestation; overgrazing; soil erosion; poaching is widespread

Environment - international agreements:

party to: Biodiversity, Climate Change, Desertification, Endangered Species, Hazardous Wastes, Law of the Sea, Marine Life Conservation, Nuclear Test Ban, Ozone Layer Protection, Wetlands

signed, but not ratified: Environmental Modification

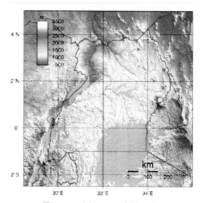

Topographic map of Uganda

See also

- List of national parks of Uganda

Languages

English language

English		
Pronunciation	/ˈɪŋɡlɪʃ/	
Spoken in	(see below)	
Total speakers	First language: 309–400 million Second language: 199–1,400 million Overall: 500 million–1.8 billion	
Ranking	3 (native speakers) Total: 1 or 2	

Language family	Indo-European
	
	• Germanic
	
	  • West Germanic
	
	    • Anglo–Frisian
	
	      • Anglic
	
	        • English	

Writing system	Latin (English variant)	
Official status		
Official language in	53 countries United Nations European Union Commonwealth of Nations CoE NATO NAFTA OAS OIC PIF UKUSA	
Regulated by	*No official regulation*	
Language codes		
ISO 639-1	en	

ISO 639-2	eng
ISO 639-3	eng [1]
Linguasphere	52-ABA

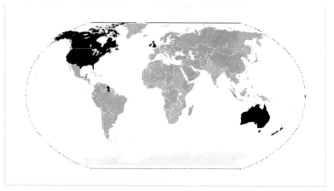

Countries where English is a majority language.   Countries where English is an official but not a majority language.

English is a West Germanic language that arose in the Anglo-Saxon kingdoms of England and spread into what was to become south-east Scotland under the influence of the Anglian medieval kingdom of Northumbria. Following the economic, political, military, scientific, cultural, and colonial influence of Great Britain and the United Kingdom from the 18th century, via the British Empire, and of the United States since the mid-20th century, it has been widely dispersed around the world, become the leading language of international discourse, and has acquired use as *lingua franca* in many regions. It is widely learned as a second language and used as an official language of the European Union and many Commonwealth countries, as well as in many world organisations. It is the third most natively spoken language in the world, after Mandarin Chinese and Spanish.

Historically, English originated from the fusion of languages and dialects, now collectively termed Old English, which were brought to the eastern coast of Great Britain by Germanic (Anglo-Saxon) settlers beginning in the 5th century – with the word "English" being derived from the name of the Angles. A significant number of English words are constructed based on roots from Latin, because Latin in some form was the *lingua franca* of the Christian Church and of European intellectual life. The language was further influenced by the Old Norse language with Viking invasions in the 8th and 9th centuries.

The Norman conquest of England in the 11th century gave rise to heavy borrowings from Norman-French, and vocabulary and spelling conventions began to give the superficial appearance of a close relationship with Romance languages to what had now become Middle English. The Great Vowel Shift that began in the south of England in the 15th century is one of the historical events marking the separation of Middle and Modern English.

Owing to the significant assimilation of various European languages throughout history, modern English is often seen as having a very large vocabulary. The *Oxford English Dictionary* lists over 250,000 distinct words, and does not include many technical or slang terms, or words that belong to multiple word classes.

Significance

See also: English-speaking world and Anglosphere

Modern English, sometimes described as the first global lingua franca, is the dominant language or in some instances even the required international language of communications, science, information technology, business, aviation, entertainment, radio and diplomacy. Its spread beyond the British Isles began with the growth of the British Empire, and by the late 19th century its reach was truly global. Following the British colonisation of North America, it became the dominant language in the United States and in Canada. The growing economic and cultural influence of the US and its status as a global superpower since World War II have significantly accelerated the language's spread across the planet.

A working knowledge of English has become a requirement in a number of fields, occupations and professions such as medicine and computing; as a consequence over a billion people speak English to at least a basic level (see English language learning and teaching). It is one of six official languages of the United Nations.

One impact of the growth of English has been to reduce native linguistic diversity in many parts of the world, and its influence continues to play an important role in language attrition. Conversely the natural internal variety of English along with creoles and pidgins have the potential to produce new distinct languages from English over time.

History

Main article: History of the English language

English is a West Germanic language that originated from the Anglo-Frisian and Old Saxon dialects brought to Britain by Germanic settlers from various parts of what is now northwest Germany, Denmark and the Netherlands in the 5th century. Up to that point, in Roman Britain the native population is assumed to have spoken the Celtic language Brythonic alongside the acrolectal influence of Latin, from the 400-year Roman occupation.

One of these incoming Germanic tribes was the Angles, whom Bede believed to have relocated entirely to Britain. The names 'England' (from *Engla land* "Land of the Angles") and *English* (Old English *Englisc*) are derived from the name of this tribe—but Saxons, Jutes and a range of Germanic peoples from the coasts of Frisia, Lower Saxony, Jutland and Southern Sweden also moved to Britain in this era.

Initially, Old English was a diverse group of dialects, reflecting the varied origins of the Anglo-Saxon kingdoms of Great Britain but one of these dialects, Late West Saxon, eventually came to dominate, and it is in this that the poem *Beowulf* is written.

Old English was later transformed by two waves of invasion. The first was by speakers of the North Germanic language branch when Halfdan Ragnarsson and Ivar the Boneless started the conquering and colonisation of northern parts of the British Isles in the 8th and 9th centuries (see Danelaw). The second was by speakers of the Romance language Old Norman in the 11th century with the Norman conquest of England. Norman developed into Anglo-Norman, and then Anglo-French - and introduced a layer of words especially via the courts and government. As well as extending the lexicon with Scandinavian and Norman words these two events also simplified the grammar and transformed English into a borrowing language—more than normally open to accept new words from other languages.

The linguistic shifts in English following the Norman invasion produced what is now referred to as Middle English, with Geoffrey Chaucer's *The Canterbury Tales* being the best known work.

Throughout all this period Latin in some form was the *lingua franca* of European intellectual life, first the Medieval Latin of the Christian Church, but later the humanist Renaissance Latin, and those that wrote or copied texts in Latin commonly coined new terms from Latin to refer to things or concepts for which there was no existing native English word.

Modern English, which includes the works of William Shakespeare and the King James Bible, is generally dated from about 1550, and when the United Kingdom became a colonial power, English served as the lingua franca of the colonies of the British Empire. In the post-colonial period, some of the newly created nations which had multiple indigenous languages opted to continue using English as the lingua franca to avoid the political difficulties inherent in promoting any one indigenous language above the others. As a result of the growth of the British Empire, English was adopted in North America, India, Africa, Australia and many other regions, a trend extended with the emergence of the United States as a superpower in the mid-20th century.

Classification and related languages

The English language belongs to the Anglo-Frisian sub-group of the West Germanic branch of the Germanic family, a member of the Indo-European languages. Modern English is the direct descendant of Middle English, itself a direct descendant of Old English, a descendant of Proto-Germanic. Typical of most Germanic languages, English is characterised by the use of modal verbs, the division of verbs into strong and weak classes, and common sound shifts from Proto-Indo-European known as Grimm's Law. The closest living relatives of English are the Scots language (spoken primarily in Scotland and parts of Ireland) and Frisian (spoken on the southern fringes of the North Sea in Denmark, the Netherlands, and Germany).

After Scots and Frisian come those Germanic languages that are more distantly related: the non-Anglo-Frisian West Germanic languages (Dutch, Afrikaans, Low German, High German), and the North Germanic languages (Swedish, Danish, Norwegian, Icelandic, and Faroese). With the exception of Scots, none of the other languages is mutually intelligible with English, owing in part to the divergences in lexis, syntax, semantics, and phonology, and to the isolation afforded to the English language by the British Isles, although some such as Dutch do show strong affinities with English, especially to earlier stages of the language. Isolation has allowed English and Scots (as well as Icelandic and Faroese) to develop independently of the Continental Germanic languages and their influences over time.

In addition to isolation, lexical differences between English and other Germanic languages exist due to heavy borrowing in English of words from Latin and French. For example, we say "exit" (Latin), vs. Dutch *uitgang*, literally "out-going" (though *outgang* survives dialectally in restricted usage) and "change" (French) vs. German *Änderung* (literally "alteration, othering"); "movement" (French) vs. German *Bewegung* ("be-way-ing", i.e. "proceeding along the way"); etc. Preference of one synonym over another also causes differentiation in lexis, even where both words are Germanic, as in English *care* vs. German *Sorge*. Both words descend from Proto-Germanic **karo* and **surgo* respectively, but **karo* has become the dominant word in English for "care" while in German, Dutch, and Scandinavian languages, the **surgo* root prevailed. **Surgo* still survives in English, however, as *sorrow*.

Although the syntax of English is significantly different from that of German and other West Germanic languages, with different rules for setting up sentences (for example, German *Ich **habe** nie etwas auf dem Platz **gesehen*** and the Dutch *Ik **heb** nooit iets op het plein **gezien*** vs. English "I **have** never **seen** anything in the square"), English syntax remains extremely similar to that of the North Germanic languages, which are believed to have influenced English syntax during the Middle English Period (e.g., Danish *Jeg **har** aldrig **set** noget på torvet*; Icelandic *Ég **hef** aldrei **séð** neitt á torginu*).

The kinship with other Germanic languages can be seen in the large amount of cognates (e.g. Dutch *zenden*, German *senden*, English *send*; Dutch *goud*, German *Gold*, English *gold*, etc.). It also gives rise to false friends, see for example English *time* vs Norwegian *time* ("hour"), and differences in phonology can obscure words that really are related (*tooth* vs. German *Zahn*; compare also Danish *tand*). Sometimes both semantics *and* phonology are different (German *Zeit* ("time") is related to English "tide", but the English word, through a transitional phase of meaning "period"/"interval", has come primarily to mean gravitational effects on the ocean by the moon, though the original meaning is preserved in forms like *tidings* and *betide*, and phrases such as *to tide over*).[citation needed]

Many North Germanic words also entered English due to the settlement of Viking raiders and Danish invasions which began around the 9th century (see Danelaw). Many of these words are common words, often mistaken for being native, which shows how close-knit the relations between the English and the Scandinavian settlers were. These include such common words as *anger, awe, bag, big, birth, blunder, both, cake, call, cast, cosy, cut, die, dirt, drag, drown, egg, fellow, flat, flounder, gain, get, gift, give, guess, guest, gust, hug, husband, ill, kid, law, leg, lift, likely, link, loan, loose, low, mistake, odd, race (running), raise, root, rotten, same, scale, scare, score, seat, seem, sister, skill, skin, skirt, skull, sky, stain, steak, sway, take, though, thrive, Thursday, tight, till (until), trust, ugly, want, weak, window, wing, wrong,* and even the pronoun *they* (and its forms) and possibly *are* (the present plural form of *to be*).[citation needed] More recent Scandinavian imports include *angstrom, fjord, geyser, kraken, litmus, nickel, ombudsman, saga, ski, slalom, smorgasbord, and tungsten.* Dutch and Low German also had a considerable influence on English vocabulary, contributing common everyday terms and many nautical and trading terms (*See below: Word Origins: Dutch and Low German origins*).

Finally, English has been forming compound words and affixing existing words separately from the other Germanic languages for over 1500 years and has different habits in that regard. For instance, abstract nouns in English may be formed from native words by the suffixes "-hood", "-ship", "-dom" and "-ness". All of these have cognate suffixes in most or all other Germanic languages, but their usage patterns have diverged, as German "Freiheit" vs. English "freedom" (the suffix "-heit" being cognate of English "-hood", while English "-dom" is cognate with German "-tum"). The Germanic languages Icelandic and Faroese also follow English in this respect, since, like English, they developed independent of German influences.

Many French words are also intelligible to an English speaker, especially when they are seen in writing (as pronunciations are often quite different), because English absorbed a large vocabulary from Norman and French, via Anglo-Norman after the Norman Conquest, and directly from French in subsequent centuries. As a result, a large portion of English vocabulary is derived from French, with some minor spelling differences (e.g. inflectional endings, use of old French spellings, lack of diacritics, etc.), as well as occasional divergences in meaning of so-called false friends: for example, compare "library" with the French *librairie*, which means bookstore; in French, the word for "library" is *bibliothèque*. The pronunciation of most French loanwords in English (with the exception of a handful of more recently borrowed words such as *mirage, genre, café;* or phrases like *coup d'état, rendez-vous,* etc.) has become largely anglicised and follows a typically English phonology and pattern of stress (compare English "nature" vs. French *nature*, "button" vs. *bouton*, "table" vs. *table*, "hour" vs. *heure*, "reside" vs. *résider*, etc.).[citation needed]

Geographical distribution

See also: List of countries by English-speaking population

Approximately 375 million people speak English as their first language. English today is probably the third largest language by number of native speakers, after Mandarin Chinese and Spanish. However, when combining native and non-native speakers it is probably the most commonly spoken language in the world, though possibly second to a combination of the Chinese languages (depending on whether or not distinctions in the latter are classified as "languages" or "dialects").

Estimates that include second language speakers vary greatly from 470 million to over a billion depending on how literacy or mastery is defined and measured. Linguistics professor David Crystal calculates that non-native speakers now outnumber native speakers by a ratio of 3 to 1.

Pie chart showing the relative numbers of native English speakers in the major English-speaking countries of the world

The countries with the highest populations of native English speakers are, in descending order: United States (215 million), United Kingdom (61 million), Canada (18.2 million), Australia (15.5 million), Nigeria (4 million), Ireland (3.8 million), South Africa (3.7 million), and New Zealand (3.6 million) 2006 Census.

Countries such as the Philippines, Jamaica and Nigeria also have millions of native speakers of dialect continua ranging from an English-based creole to a more standard version of English. Of those nations where English is spoken as a second language, India has the most such speakers ('Indian English'). Crystal claims that, combining native and non-native speakers, India now has more people who speak or understand English than any other country in the world.

Countries in order of total speakers

Country	Total	Percent of population	First language	As an additional language	Population	Comment
United States of America	251,388,301	96%	215,423,557	35,964,744	262,375,152	Source: US Census 2000: Language Use and English-Speaking Ability: 2000 [2]. Table 1. Figure for second language speakers are respondents who reported they do not speak English at home but know it "very well" or "well". Note: figures are for population age 5 and older

India	125,344,736	12%	226,449	86,125,221 second language speakers. 38,993,066 third language speakers	1,028,737,436	Figures include both those who speak English as a *second language* and those who speak it as a *third language*. 2001 figures. The figures include English *speakers*, but not English *users*.
Nigeria	79,000,000	53%	4,000,000	>75,000,000	148,000,000	Figures are for speakers of Nigerian Pidgin, an English-based pidgin or creole. Ihemere gives a range of roughly 3 to 5 million native speakers; the midpoint of the range is used in the table. Ihemere, Kelechukwu Uchechukwu. 2006. "A Basic Description and Analytic Treatment of Noun Clauses in Nigerian Pidgin. [3]" *Nordic Journal of African Studies* 15(3): 296–313.
United Kingdom	59,600,000	98%	58,100,000	1,500,000	60,000,000	Source: Crystal (2005), p. 109.
Philippines	48,800,000	58%	3,427,000	43,974,000	84,566,000	Total speakers: Census 2000, text above Figure 7 [4]. 63.71% of the 66.7 million people aged 5 years or more could speak English. Native speakers: Census 1995, as quoted by Andrew González in The Language Planning Situation in the Philippines [5], Journal of Multilingual and Multicultural Development, 19 (5&6), 487–525. (1998). Ethnologue lists 3.4 million native speakers with 52% of the population speaking it as a additional language.
Canada	25,246,220	85%	17,694,830	7,551,390	29,639,030	Source: 2001 Census – Knowledge of Official Languages [6] and Mother Tongue [7]. The native speakers figure comprises 122,660 people with both French and English as a mother tongue, plus 17,572,170 people with English and not French as a mother tongue.

Australia	18,172,989	92%	15,581,329	2,591,660	19,855,288	Source: 2006 Census. The figure shown in the first language English speakers column is actually the number of Australian residents who speak only English at home. The additional language column shows the number of other residents who claim to speak English "well" or "very well". Another 5% of residents did not state their home language or English proficiency.
Note: Total = First language + Other language; Percentage = Total / Population						

Countries where English is a major language

English is the primary language in Anguilla, Antigua and Barbuda, Australia, the Bahamas, Barbados, Belize, Bermuda, the British Indian Ocean Territory, the British Virgin Islands, Canada, the Cayman Islands, Dominica, the Falkland Islands, Gibraltar, Grenada, Guam, Guernsey, Guyana, Ireland , The Isle of Man, Jamaica, Jersey, Montserrat, Nauru, New Zealand, Pitcairn Islands, Saint Helena, Saint Kitts and Nevis, Saint Vincent and the Grenadines, Singapore, South Georgia and the South Sandwich Islands, Trinidad and Tobago, the Turks and Caicos Islands, the United Kingdom and the United States.

In some countries where English is not the most spoken language, it is an official language; these countries include Botswana, Cameroon, the Federated States of Micronesia, Fiji, Gambia, Ghana, India, Kenya, Kiribati, Lesotho, Liberia, Madagascar, Malta, the Marshall Islands, Mauritius, Namibia, Nigeria, Pakistan, Palau, Papua New Guinea, the Philippines (Philippine English), Rwanda, Saint Lucia, Samoa, Seychelles, Sierra Leone, the Solomon Islands, Sri Lanka, the Sudan, Swaziland, Tanzania, Uganda, Zambia, and Zimbabwe.

It is also one of the 11 official languages that are given equal status in South Africa (South African English). English is also the official language in current dependent territories of Australia (Norfolk Island, Christmas Island and Cocos Island) and of the United States (American Samoa, Guam, Northern Mariana Islands, Puerto Rico, and the U.S. Virgin Islands), and the former British colony of Hong Kong. (See List of countries where English is an official language for more details.)

English is not an official language in either the United States or the United Kingdom. Although the United States federal government has no official languages, English has been given official status by 30 of the 50 state governments. Although falling short of official status, English is also an important language in several former colonies and protectorates of the United Kingdom, such as Bahrain, Bangladesh, Brunei, Malaysia, and the United Arab Emirates. English is not an official language of Israel, but is taken as a required second language at all Jewish and Arab schools and therefore widely spoken.

English as a global language

See also: English in computing, International English, and World language

Because English is so widely spoken, it has often been referred to as a "world language", the *lingua franca* of the modern era, and while it is not an official language in most countries, it is currently the language most often taught as a foreign language. Some linguists believe that it is no longer the exclusive cultural property of "native English speakers", but is rather a language that is absorbing aspects of cultures worldwide as it continues to grow. It is, by international treaty, the official language for aerial and maritime communications. English is an official language of the United Nations and many other international organisations, including the International Olympic Committee.

English is the language most often studied as a foreign language in the European Union, by 89% of schoolchildren, ahead of French at 32%, while the perception of the usefulness of foreign languages amongst Europeans is 68% in favour of English ahead of 25% for French. Among some non-English speaking EU countries, a large percentage of the adult population can converse in English — in particular: 85% in Sweden, 83% in Denmark, 79% in the Netherlands, 66% in Luxembourg and over 50% in Finland, Slovenia, Austria, Belgium, and Germany.

Books, magazines, and newspapers written in English are available in many countries around the world, and English is the most commonly used language in the sciences with Science Citation Index reporting as early as 1997 that 95% of its articles were written in English, even though only half of them came from authors in English-speaking countries.

This increasing use of the English language globally has had a large impact on many other languages, leading to language shift and even language death, and to claims of linguistic imperialism. English itself is now open to language shift as multiple regional varieties feed back into the language as a whole. For this reason, the 'English language is forever evolving'.

Dialects and regional varieties

Main article: List of dialects of the English language

The expansion of the British Empire and—since World War II—the influence of the United States have spread English throughout the globe. Because of that global spread, English has developed a host of English dialects and English-based creole languages and pidgins.

Several educated native dialects of English have wide acceptance as standards in much of the world, with much emphasis placed on one dialect based on educated southern British and another based on educated Midwestern American. The former is sometimes called BBC (or the Queen's) English, and it may be noticeable by its preference for "Received Pronunciation". The latter dialect, General American, which is spread over most of the United States and much of Canada, is more typically the model for the American continents and areas (such as the Philippines) that have had either close association with the United States, or a desire to be so identified. In Oceania, the major native dialect of

Australian English is spoken as a first language by 92% of the inhabitants of the Australian continent, with General Australian serving as the standard accent. The English of neighbouring New Zealand as well as that of South Africa have to a lesser degree been influential native varieties of the language.

Aside from these major dialects, there are numerous other varieties of English, which include, in most cases, several subvarieties, such as Cockney, Scouse and Geordie within British English; Newfoundland English within Canadian English; and African American Vernacular English ("Ebonics") and Southern American English within American English. English is a pluricentric language, without a central language authority like France's Académie française; and therefore no one variety is considered "correct" or "incorrect" except in terms of the expectations of the particular audience to which the language is directed.

Scots has its origins in early Northern Middle English and developed and changed during its history with influence from other sources, but following the Acts of Union 1707 a process of language attrition began, whereby successive generations adopted more and more features from Standard English, causing dialectalisation. Whether it is now a separate language or a dialect of English better described as Scottish English is in dispute, although the UK government now accepts Scots as a regional language and has recognised it as such under the European Charter for Regional or Minority Languages. There are a number of regional dialects of Scots, and pronunciation, grammar and lexis of the traditional forms differ, sometimes substantially, from other varieties of English.

English speakers have many different accents, which often signal the speaker's native dialect or language. For the more distinctive characteristics of regional accents, see Regional accents of English, and for the more distinctive characteristics of regional dialects, see List of dialects of the English language. Within England, variation is now largely confined to pronunciation rather than grammar or vocabulary. At the time of the Survey of English Dialects, grammar and vocabulary differed across the country, but a process of *lexical attrition* has led most of this variation to die out.

Just as English itself has borrowed words from many different languages over its history, English loanwords now appear in many languages around the world, indicative of the technological and cultural influence of its speakers. Several pidgins and creole languages have been formed on an English base, such as Jamaican Patois, Nigerian Pidgin, and Tok Pisin. There are many words in English coined to describe forms of particular non-English languages that contain a very high proportion of English words.

Constructed varieties of English

- Basic English is simplified for easy international use. Manufacturers and other international businesses tend to write manuals and communicate in Basic English. Some English schools in Asia teach it as a practical subset of English for use by beginners.
- E-Prime excludes forms of the verb *to be*.
- English reform is an attempt to improve collectively upon the English language.
- Manually Coded English constitutes a variety of systems that have been developed to represent the English language with hand signals, designed primarily for use in deaf education. These should not be confused with true sign languages such as British Sign Language and American Sign Language used in Anglophone countries, which are independent and not based on English.
- Seaspeak and the related Airspeak and Policespeak, all based on restricted vocabularies, were designed by Edward Johnson in the 1980s to aid international cooperation and communication in specific areas. There is also a tunnelspeak for use in the Channel Tunnel.
- Simplified Technical English was historically developed for aerospace industry maintenance manuals and is now used in various industries.
- Special English is a simplified version of English used by the Voice of America. It uses a vocabulary of only 1500 words.

Phonology

Main article: English phonology

Vowels

See also: IPA chart for English dialects

It is the vowels that differ most from region to region. Length is not phonemic in most varieties of North American English.

IPA	Description	word
monophthongs		
iː	Close front unrounded vowel	bead
ɪ	Near-close near-front unrounded vowel	bid
ɛ	Open-mid front unrounded vowel	bed
æ	Near-open front unrounded vowel	bad

ɒ	Open back rounded vowel	box
ɔː	Open-mid back rounded vowel	pawed
ɑː	Open back unrounded vowel	bra
ʊ	Near-close near-back vowel	good
uː	Close back rounded vowel	booed
ʌ	Open-mid back unrounded vowel, near-open central vowel	bud
ɜr	Open-mid central unrounded vowel	bird
ə	Schwa	Rosa's
ɨ	Close central unrounded vowel	roses
diphthongs		
eɪ	Close-mid front unrounded vowel- Close front unrounded vowel	bayed
oʊ	Close-mid back rounded vowel- Near-close near-back vowel	bode
aɪ	Open front unrounded vowel Near-close near-front unrounded vowel	cry This is near-universal in Canada, and most non-Southern American English dialects also have undergone the shift; in the 2008 presidential election, both candidates as well as their vice-presidents all used [ʌɪ] for the word "right". [citation needed]
aʊ	Open front unrounded vowel Near-close near-back vowel	cow
ɔɪ	Open-mid back rounded vowel Close front unrounded vowel	boy
ʊər	Near-close near-back vowel Schwa	boor

ɛər	Open-mid front unrounded vowel Schwa	fair

Consonants

This is the English consonantal system using symbols from the International Phonetic Alphabet (IPA).

	Bilabial	Labio-dental	Dental	Alveolar	Post-alveolar	Palatal	Velar	Labial-velar	Glottal
Nasal	m			n			ŋ		
Plosive	p b			t d			k g		
Affricate					tʃ dʒ				
Fricative		f v	θ ð	s z	ʃ ʒ	ç	x		h
Flap					ɾ				
Approximant				ɹ		j		ʍ w	
Lateral				l					

Voicing and aspiration

Voicing and aspiration of stop consonants in English depend on dialect and context, but a few general rules can be given:

- Voiceless plosives and affricates (/p/, /t/, /k/, and /tʃ/) are aspirated when they are word-initial or begin a stressed syllable – compare *pin* [pʰɪn] and *spin* [spɪn], *crap* [kʰɹæp] and *scrap* [skɹæp].
  - In some dialects, aspiration extends to unstressed syllables as well.
  - In other dialects, such as Indian English, all voiceless stops remain unaspirated.
- Word-initial voiced plosives may be devoiced in some dialects.
- Word-terminal voiceless plosives may be unreleased or accompanied by a glottal stop in some dialects; examples: *tap* [tʰæp̚], *sack* [sæk̚].
- Word-terminal voiced plosives may be devoiced in some dialects (e.g. some varieties of American English) – examples: *sad* [sæd̥], *bag* [bæɪɡ̊]. In other dialects, they are fully voiced in final position, but only partially voiced in initial position.

Supra-segmental features

Tone groups

English is an intonation language. This means that the pitch of the voice is used syntactically; for example, to convey surprise or irony, or to change a statement into a question.

In English, intonation patterns are on groups of words, which are called tone groups, tone units, intonation groups, or sense groups. Tone groups are said on a single breath and, as a consequence, are of limited length, more often being on average five words long or lasting roughly two seconds. For example:

/duː juː ˈniːd ˈɛnɪθɪŋ/ *Do you need anything?*

/aɪ ˈdoʊnt | ˈnoʊ/ *I don't, no*

/aɪ doʊnt ˈnoʊ/ *I don't know* (contracted to, for example, [ˈaɪ doʊnoʊ] or [ˈaɪdənoʊ] *I dunno* in fast or colloquial speech that de-emphasises the pause between 'don't' and 'know' even further)

Characteristics of intonation—stress

English is a strongly stressed language, in that certain syllables, both within words and within phrases, get a relative prominence/loudness during pronunciation while the others do not. The former kind of syllables are said to be *accentuated/stressed* and the latter are *unaccentuated/unstressed*. Stress can also be used in English to distinguish between certain verbs and their noun counterparts. For example, in the case of the verb *contract*, the second syllable is stressed: /kɒnˈtrækt/; in case of the corresponding noun, the first syllable is stressed: /ˈkɒn.trækt/. Vowels in unstressed syllables can also change in quality, hence the verb *contract* often becomes (and indeed is listed in Oxford English Dictionary as) /kənˈtrækt/. In each word, there can be only one principal stress, but in long words, there can be secondary stress(es) too, e.g. in *civilisation* /ˌsɪ.və.laɪˈzeɪ.ʃn̩/, the 1st syllable carries the secondary stress, the 4th syllable carries the primary stress, and the other syllables are unstressed.

Hence in a sentence, each tone group can be subdivided into syllables, which can either be stressed (strong) or unstressed (weak). The stressed syllable is called the nuclear syllable. For example:

*That | was | the | **best** | thing | you | could | have | **done**!*

Here, all syllables are unstressed, except the syllables/words *best* and *done*, which are stressed. *Best* is stressed harder and, therefore, is the nuclear syllable.

The nuclear syllable carries the main point the speaker wishes to make. For example:

John had not stolen that money. (... Someone else had.)

John *had not* stolen that money. (... Someone said he had. or... Not at that time, but later he did.)

John had not *stolen* that money. (... He acquired the money by some other means.)

John had not stolen *that* money. (... He had stolen some other money.)

John had not stolen that *money*. (... He had stolen something else.)

Also

I did not tell her that. (... Someone else told her)

I *did not* tell her that. (... You said I did. or... but now I will)

I did not *tell* her that. (... I did not say it; she could have inferred it, etc)

I did not tell *her* that. (... I told someone else)

I did not tell her *that*. (... I told her something else)

This can also be used to express emotion:

Oh, really? (...I did not know that)

Oh, *really*? (...I disbelieve you. or... That is blatantly obvious)

The nuclear syllable is spoken more loudly than the others and has a characteristic change of pitch. The changes of pitch most commonly encountered in English are the rising pitch and the falling pitch, although the fall-rising pitch and/or the rise-falling pitch are sometimes used. In this opposition between falling and rising pitch, which plays a larger role in English than in most other languages, falling pitch conveys certainty and rising pitch uncertainty. This can have a crucial impact on meaning, specifically in relation to polarity, the positive–negative opposition; thus, falling pitch means, "polarity known", while rising pitch means "polarity unknown". This underlies the rising pitch of yes/no questions. For example:

When do you want to be paid?

Now? (Rising pitch. In this case, it denotes a question: "Can I be paid now?" or "Do you desire to pay now?")

Now. (Falling pitch. In this case, it denotes a statement: "I choose to be paid now.")

Grammar

Main article: English grammar

English grammar has minimal inflection compared with most other Indo-European languages. For example, Modern English, unlike Modern German or Dutch and the Romance languages, lacks grammatical gender and adjectival agreement. Case marking has almost disappeared from the language and mainly survives in pronouns. The patterning of strong (e.g. *speak/spoke/spoken*) versus weak verbs (e.g. *love/loved or kick/kicked*) inherited from its Germanic origins has declined in importance in modern English, and the remnants of inflection (such as plural marking) have become more regular.

At the same time, the language has become more analytic, and has developed features such as modal verbs and word order as resources for conveying meaning. Auxiliary verbs mark constructions such as questions, negative polarity, the passive voice and progressive aspect.

Vocabulary

The English vocabulary has changed considerably over the centuries.

Like many languages deriving from Proto-Indo-European (PIE), many of the most common words in English can trace back their origin (through the Germanic branch) to PIE. Such words include the basic pronouns *I*, from Old English *ic*, (cf. German *Ich*, Gothic *ik*, Latin *ego*, Greek *ego*, Sanskrit *aham*), *me* (cf. German *mich, mir*, Gothic *mik, mīs*, Latin *me*, Greek *eme*, Sanskrit *mam*), numbers (e.g. *one, two, three*, cf. Dutch *een, twee, drie*, Gothic *ains, twai, threis (þreis)*, Latin *unus, duo, tres*, Greek *oinos* "ace (on dice)", *duo, treis*), common family relationships such as mother, father, brother, sister etc. (cf. Dutch *moeder*, Greek *meter*, Latin *mater*, Sanskrit *matr; mother*), names of many animals (cf. German *Maus*, Dutch *muis*, Sankrit *mus*, Greek *mys*, Latin *mus; mouse*), and many common verbs (cf. Old High German *knājan*, Old Norse *knā*, Greek *gignōmi*, Latin *gnoscere*, Hittite *kanes; to know*).

Germanic words (generally words of Old English or to a lesser extent Old Norse origin) tend to be shorter than Latinate words in Modern English, and are more common in ordinary speech, and include nearly all the basic pronouns, prepositions, conjunctions, modal verbs etc. that form the basis of English syntax and grammar. The shortness of the words is generally due to syncope in Middle English (e.g. OldEng *hēafod* > ModEng *head*, OldEng *sāwol* > ModEng *soul*) and to the loss of final syllables due to stress (e.g. OldEng *gamen* > ModEng *game*, OldEng *ærende* > ModEng *errand*), not because Germanic words are inherently shorter than Latinate words. (The lengthier, higher-register words of Old English were largely forgotten following the subjugation of English after the Norman Conquest, and most of the Old English lexis devoted to literature, the arts, and sciences ceased to be productive when it fell into disuse. Only the shorter, more direct, words of Old English tended to pass into the Modern language.) Longer Latinate words in Modern English are often regarded as more elegant or educated. However, the excessive use of Latinate words is considered at times to be either pretentious or an attempt to obfuscate an issue. George Orwell's essay "Politics and the English Language", considered an important scrutinisation of the English language, is critical of this, as well as other perceived misuse of the language.

An English speaker is in many cases able to choose between Germanic and Latinate synonyms: *come* or *arrive*; *sight* or *vision*; *freedom* or *liberty*. In some cases, there is a choice between a Germanic derived word (*oversee*), a Latin derived word (*supervise*), and a French word derived from the same Latin word (*survey*); or even words derived from Norman French (e.g., *warranty*) and Parisian French (*guarantee*), and even choices involving multiple Germanic and Latinate sources are possible: *sickness* (Old English), *ill* (Old Norse), *infirmity* (French), *affliction* (Latin). Such synonyms harbor a variety of different meanings and nuances, enabling the speaker to express fine variations or shades of thought. Yet the ability to choose between multiple synonyms is not a consequence of French and Latin influence, as this same richness existed in English prior to the extensive borrowing of French and Latin terms. Old English was extremely resourceful in its ability to express synonyms and shades of meaning on its own, in many respects rivaling or exceeding that of Modern English (synonyms numbering in the thirties for certain concepts were not uncommon). Take for instance the various ways to express the word "astronomer" or "astrologer" in Old English: *tunglere, tungolcræftiga, tungolwītega, tīdymbwlātend, tīdscēawere*. In Modern English, however, the role of such synonyms has largely been replaced in favour of equivalents taken from Latin, French, and Greek. Familiarity with the etymology of groups of synonyms can give English speakers greater control over their linguistic register. See: List of Germanic and Latinate equivalents in English, Doublet (linguistics).

An exception to this and a peculiarity perhaps unique to a handful of languages, English included, is that the nouns for meats are commonly different from, and unrelated to, those for the animals from which they are produced, the animal commonly having a Germanic name and the meat having a French-derived one. Examples include: *deer* and *venison*; *cow* and *beef*; *swine/pig* and *pork*; and *sheep/lamb* and *mutton*. This is assumed to be a result of the aftermath of the Norman invasion, where an Anglo-Norman-speaking elite were the consumers of the meat, produced by lower classes, which happened to be largely Anglo-Saxon [citation needed], though this same duality can also be seen in other languages like French, which did not undergo such linguistic upheaval (e.g. *boeuf* "beef" vs. *vache* "cow"). With the exception of *beef* and *pork*, the distinction today is gradually becoming less and less pronounced (*venison* is commonly referred to simply as *deer meat*, *mutton* is *lamb*, and *chicken* is both the animal and the meat over the more traditional term *poultry*).

There are Latinate words that are used in everyday speech. These words no longer appear Latinate and oftentimes have no Germanic equivalents. For instance, the words *mountain, valley, river, aunt, uncle, move, use, push* and *stay ("to remain")* are Latinate. Likewise, the inverse can occur: *acknowledge, meaningful, understanding, mindful, behaviour, forbearance, behoove, forestall, allay, rhyme, starvation, embodiment* come from Anglo-Saxon, and *allegiance, abandonment, debutant, feudalism, seizure, guarantee, disregard, wardrobe, disenfranchise, disarray, bandolier, bourgeoisie, debauchery, performance, furniture, gallantry* are of Germanic origin, usually through the Germanic element in French, so it is oftentimes impossible to know the origin of a word based on its register.

English easily accepts technical terms into common usage and often imports new words and phrases. Examples of this phenomenon include contemporary words such as *cookie, Internet* and *URL* (technical terms), as well as *genre, über, lingua franca* and *amigo* (imported words/phrases from French, German, Italian, and Spanish, respectively). In addition, slang often provides new meanings for old words and phrases. In fact, this fluidity is so pronounced that a distinction often needs to be made between formal forms of English and contemporary usage.

See also: sociolinguistics

Number of words in English

The *General Explanations* at the beginning of the *Oxford English Dictionary* states:

> The Vocabulary of a widely diffused and highly cultivated living language is not a fixed quantity circumscribed by definite limits... there is absolutely no defining line in any direction: the circle of the English language has a well-defined centre but no discernible circumference.

The current FAQ for the *OED* further states:

> How many words are there in the English language? There is no single sensible answer to this question. It's impossible to count the number of words in a language, because it's so hard to decide what actually counts as a word.

The vocabulary of English is undoubtedly vast, but assigning a specific number to its size is more a matter of definition than of calculation. Unlike other languages such as French (the Académie française), German (Rat für deutsche Rechtschreibung), Spanish (Real Academia Española) and Italian (Accademia della Crusca), there is no academy to define officially accepted words and spellings. Neologisms are coined regularly in medicine, science, technology and other fields, and new slang is constantly developed. Some of these new words enter wide usage; others remain restricted to small circles. Foreign words used in immigrant communities often make their way into wider English usage. Archaic, dialectal, and regional words might or might not be widely considered as "English".

The *Oxford English Dictionary*, 2nd edition *(OED2)* includes over 600,000 definitions, following a rather inclusive policy:

> It embraces not only the standard language of literature and conversation, whether current at the moment, or obsolete, or archaic, but also the main technical vocabulary, and a large measure of dialectal usage and slang (Supplement to the *OED*, 1933).

The editors of *Webster's Third New International Dictionary, Unabridged* (475,000 main headwords) in their preface, estimate the number to be much higher. It is estimated that about 25,000 words are added to the language each year.

The Global Language Monitor announced that the English language had crossed the 1,000,000-word threshold on June 10, 2009. The announcement was met with strong scepticism by linguists and lexicographers, though a number of non-specialist reports accepted the figure uncritically.

Comparisons of the vocabulary size of English to that of other languages are generally not taken very seriously by linguists and lexicographers. Besides the fact that dictionaries will vary in their policies for including and counting entries, what is meant by a given language and what counts as a word do not have simple definitions. Also, a definition of word that works for one language may not work well in another, with differences in morphology and orthography making cross-linguistic definitions and word-counting difficult, and potentially giving very different results. Linguist Geoffrey K. Pullum has gone so far as to compare concerns over vocabulary size (and the notion that a supposedly larger lexicon leads to "greater richness and precision") to an obsession with penis length.

Word origins

Main article: Lists of English words of international origin

One of the consequences of the French influence is that the vocabulary of English is, to a certain extent, divided between those words that are Germanic (mostly West Germanic, with a smaller influence from the North Germanic branch) and those that are "Latinate" (derived directly from Latin, or through Norman French or other Romance languages). The situation is further compounded, as French, particularly Old French and Anglo-French, were also contributors in English of significant numbers of Germanic words, mostly from the Frankish element in French (see *List of English Latinates of Germanic origin*).

The majority (83%) of the 1,000 most common English words, and all of the 100 most common, are Germanic. However, the majority of more advanced words in subjects such as the sciences, philosophy and maths come from Latin or Greek, with Arabic also providing many words in astronomy, mathematics, and chemistry.

Source of the most frequent 7,476 English words

	1st 100	1st 1,000	2nd 1,000	then on
Germanic	97%	57%	39%	36%
Italic	3%	36%	51%	51%
Hellenic	0	4%	4%	7%
Others	0	3%	6%	6%

Source: Nation 2001, p. 265

Numerous sets of statistics have been proposed to demonstrate the proportionate origins of English vocabulary. None, as of yet, is considered definitive by most linguists.

A computerised survey of about 80,000 words in the old *Shorter Oxford Dictionary* (3rd ed.) was published in *Ordered Profusion* by Thomas Finkenstaedt and Dieter Wolff (1973) that estimated the origin of English words as follows:

- *Langue d'oïl*, including French and Old Norman: 28.3%
- Latin, including modern scientific and technical Latin: 28.24%
- Germanic languages (including words directly inherited from Old English; does not include Germanic words coming from the Germanic element in French, Latin or other Romance languages): 25%
- Greek: 5.32%
- No etymology given: 4.03%
- Derived from proper names: 3.28%
- All other languages: less than 1%

A survey by Joseph M. Williams in *Origins of the English Language* of 10,000 words taken from several thousand business letters gave this set of statistics:

- French (langue d'oïl): 41%
- "Native" English: 33%
- Latin: 15%
- Old Norse: 2%
- Dutch: 1%
- Other: 10%

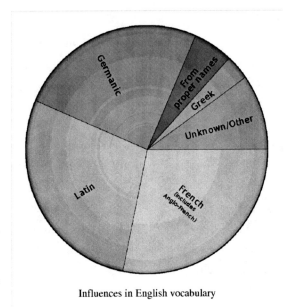

Influences in English vocabulary

Dutch and Low German origins

Main article: List of English words of Dutch origin

Many words describing the navy, types of ships, and other objects or activities on the water are of Dutch origin. *Yacht* (*jacht*), *skipper* (*schipper*), *cruiser* (*kruiser*), *flag* (*vlag*), *freight* (*vracht*), *furlough* (*verlof*), *breeze* (*bries*), *hoist* (*hijsen*), *iceberg* (*ijsberg*), *boom* (*boom*), and *maelstrom* (*maalstroom*) are examples. Other words pertain to art and daily life: *easel* (*ezel*), *etch* (*etsen*), *slim* (*slim*), *staple* (Middle Dutch *stapel* "market"), *slip* (Middle Dutch *slippen*), *landscape* (*landschap*), *cookie* (*koekje*), *curl* (*krul*), *shock* (*schokken*), *aloof* (*loef*), *boss* (*baas*), *brawl* (*brallen* "to boast"), *smack* (*smakken* "to hurl down"), *coleslaw* (*koolsla*), *dope* (*doop* "dipping sauce"), *slender* (Old Dutch *slinder*), *slight* (Middle Dutch *slicht*), *gas* (*gas*). Dutch has also contributed to English slang, e.g. *spook*, and the now obsolete *snyder* (tailor) and *stiver* (small coin).

Words from Low German include *trade* (Middle Low German *trade*), *smuggle* (*smuggeln*), and *dollar* (*daler/thaler*).

French origins

Main article: List of French words and phrases used by English speakers

A large portion of English vocabulary is of French or Langues d'oïl origin, and was transmitted to English via the Anglo-Norman language spoken by the upper classes in England in the centuries following the Norman Conquest. Words of French origin include *competition, mountain, art, table, publicity, police, role, routine, machine, force,* and thousands of others, most of which have been anglicised to fit English rules of phonology, pronunciation and spelling, rather than those of French (with a few exceptions, for example, façade and affaire de cœur.)

Writing system

Main articles: English alphabet and English orthography

Since around the 9th century, English has been written in the Latin alphabet, which replaced Anglo-Saxon runes. The spelling system, or orthography, is multilayered, with elements of French, Latin and Greek spelling on top of the native Germanic system; it has grown to vary significantly from the phonology of the language. The spelling of words often diverges considerably from how they are spoken.

Though letters and sounds may not correspond in isolation, spelling rules that take into account syllable structure, phonetics, and accents are 75% or more reliable. Some phonics spelling advocates claim that English is more than 80% phonetic. However, English has fewer consistent relationships between sounds and letters than many other languages; for example, the letter sequence *ough* can be pronounced in 10 different ways. The consequence of this complex orthographic history is that reading can be challenging.

It takes longer for students to become completely fluent readers of English than of many other languages, including French, Greek, and Spanish. "English-speaking children take up to two years more to learn reading than do children in 12 other European countries."(Professor Philip H K Seymour, University of Dundee, 2001) "[dyslexia] is twice as prevalent among dyslexics in the United States (and France) as it is among Italian dyslexics. Again, this is seen to be because of Italian's 'transparent' orthography." (Eraldo Paulesu and 11 others. Science, 2001) There are many individuals and organisationsWikipedia:Avoid weasel words whose aim is to modernise or regularise English spelling.[*citation needed*]

Basic sound-letter correspondence

See also: Hard and soft C and Hard and soft G

IPA	Alphabetic representation	Dialect-specific
p	p	
b	b	
t	t, th *(rarely) thyme, Thames*	th *thing (African American, New York)*
d	d	th *that (African American, New York)*
k	c *(+ a, o, u, consonants),* k, ck, ch, qu *(rarely) conquer,* kh *(in foreign words)*	
g	g, gh, gu *(+ a, e, i),* gue *(final position)*	
m	m	
n	n	
ŋ	n *(before g or k),* ng	
f	f, ph, gh *(final, infrequent) laugh, rough*	th *thing (many forms of English language in England)*
v	v	th *with (Cockney, Estuary English)*
θ	th *thick, think, through*	
ð	th *that, this, the*	
s	s, c *(+ e, i, y),* sc *(+ e, i, y),* ç often c *(façade/facade)*	
z	z, s *(finally or occasionally medially),* ss *(rarely) possess, dessert,* word-initial x *xylophone*	
ʃ	sh, sch *(some dialects) schedule* (plus words of German origin), ti (before vowel) *portion,* ci/ce (before vowel) *suspicion, ocean;* si/ssi (before vowel) *tension, mission;* ch *(esp. in words of French origin);* rarely s/ss before u *sugar, issue;* chsi in *fuchsia* only	
ʒ	medial si (before vowel) *division,* medial s (before "ur") *pleasure,* zh *(in foreign words),* z before u *azure,* g *(in words of French origin) (+e, i, y) genre,* j *(in words of French origin) bijou*	
x	kh, ch, h *(in foreign words)*	occasionally ch *loch (Scottish English, Welsh English)*
h	h *(syllable-initially, otherwise silent),* j *(in words of Spanish origin) jai alai*	
tʃ	ch, tch, t before u *future, culture*	t *(+ u, ue, eu) tune, Tuesday, Teutonic (several dialects – see Phonological history of English consonant clusters)*

dʒ	j, g (+ e, i, y), dg (+ e, i, consonant) badge, judg(e)ment	d (+ u, ue, ew) dune, due, dew (several dialects – another example of yod coalescence)
ɹ	r, wr (initial) wrangle	
j	y (initially or surrounded by vowels), j hallelujah	
l	l	
w	w	
ʍ	wh (pronounced hw)	Scottish and Irish English, as well as some varieties of American, New Zealand, and English English

Written accents

Main article: English words with diacritics

Unlike most other Germanic languages, English has almost no diacritics except in foreign loanwords (like the acute accent in *café*), and in the uncommon use of a diaeresis mark (often in formal writing) to indicate that two vowels are pronounced separately, rather than as one sound (e.g. *naïve*, *Zoë*). Words such as *décor*, *café*, *résumé/resumé*, *entrée*, *fiancée* and *naïve* are frequently spelled both with or without diacritics.

Some English words retain diacritics to distinguish them from others, such as *animé*, *exposé*, *lamé*, *öre*, *pâté*, *piqué*, and *rosé*, though these are sometimes also dropped (for example, *résumé/resumé*, is often spelt *resume* in the United States). To clarify pronunciation, a small number of loanwords may employ a diacritic that does not appear in the original word, such as *maté*, from Spanish *yerba mate*, or *Malé*, the capital of the Maldives, following the French usage.

Formal written English

Main article: Formal written English

A version of the language almost universally agreed upon by educated English speakers around the world is called formal written English. It takes virtually the same form regardless of where it is written, in contrast to spoken English, which differs significantly between dialects, accents, and varieties of slang and of colloquial and regional expressions. Local variations in the formal written version of the language are quite limited, being restricted largely to the spelling differences between British and American English, along with a few minor differences in grammar and lexis.

Basic and simplified versions

To make English easier to read, there are some simplified versions of the language. One basic version is named *Basic English*, a constructed language with a small number of words created by Charles Kay Ogden and described in his book *Basic English: A General Introduction with Rules and Grammar* (1930). The language is based on a simplified version of English. Ogden said that it would take seven years to learn English, seven months for Esperanto, and seven weeks for Basic English. Thus, Basic English may be employed by companies that need to make complex books for international use, as well as by language schools that need to give people some knowledge of English in a short time.

Ogden did not include any words in Basic English that could be said with a combination of other words, and he worked to make the vocabulary suitable for speakers of any other language. He put his vocabulary selections through a large number of tests and adjustments. Ogden also simplified the grammar but tried to keep it normal for English users.

The concept gained its greatest publicity just after the Second World War as a tool for world peace.[*citation needed*] Although it was not built into a program, similar simplifications were devised for various international uses.

Another version, Simplified English, exists, which is a controlled language originally developed for aerospace industry maintenance manuals. It offers a carefully limited and standardised subset of English. Simplified English has a lexicon of approved words and those words can only be used in certain ways. For example, the word *close* can be used in the phrase "Close the door" but not "do not go close to the landing gear".

See also

- Changes to Old English vocabulary
- English for Academic Purposes
- English language in Europe
- English language learning and teaching
- Language Report
- Lists of English words
- Teaching English as a foreign language
- The Adventure of English (film)
- The Story of English

References

Bibliography

- Ammon, Ulrich (2006). *Sociolinguistics: an international handbook of the science of language and society* [8]. Walter de Gruyter. ISBN 3110184184.
- Baugh, Albert C.; Thomas Cable (2002). *A history of the English language* (5th ed.). Routledge. ISBN 0-415-28099-0.
- Bragg, Melvyn (2004). *The Adventure of English: The Biography of a Language*. Arcade Publishing. ISBN 1-55970-710-0.
- Cercignani, Fausto, *Shakespeare's Works and Elizabethan Pronunciation*, Oxford, Clarendon Press, 1981.
- Crystal, David (1997). *English as a Global Language* [9]. Cambridge: Cambridge University Press. ISBN 0-521-53032-6.
- Crystal, David (2003). *The Cambridge encyclopedia of the English language* (2nd ed.). Cambridge University Press. ISBN 0-521-53033-4.
- Crystal, David (2004). *The Stories of English*. Allen Lane. ISBN 0713997524.
- Halliday, MAK (1994). *An introduction to functional grammar* (2nd ed.). London: Edward Arnold. ISBN 0-340-55782-6.
- Hayford, Harrison; Howard P. Vincent (1954). *Reader and Writer*. Houghton Mifflin Company. "Internet Archive: Free Download: Reader And Writer" [10]. Archive.org. 2001-03-10. Retrieved 2010-01-02.
- Howatt, Anthony (2004). *A history of English language teaching* [11]. Oxford University Press. ISBN 0194421856.
- Kenyon, John Samuel and Knott, Thomas Albert, *A Pronouncing Dictionary of American English*, G & C Merriam Company, Springfield, Mass, USA,1953.
- Mazrui, Alamin (1998). *The power of Babel: language & governance in the African experience* [12]. University of Chicago Press. ISBN 0852558074.
- McArthur, T. (ed.) (1992). *The Oxford Companion to the English Language*. Oxford University Press. ISBN 0-19-214183-X.
- McCrum; Robert MacNeil, William Cran (1986). *The Story of English* (1st ed.). New York: Viking. ISBN 0-670-80467-3.
- Nation, I.S.P. (2001), *Learning Vocabulary in Another Language* [13], Cambridge University Press, pp. 477, ISBN 0521804981
- Plotkin, Vulf (2006). *The Language System of English*. BrownWalker Press. ISBN 1-58112-993-9.
- Robinson, Orrin (1992). *Old English and Its Closest Relatives*. Stanford Univ. Press. ISBN 0-8047-2221-8.
- Schneider, Edgar (2007). *Postcolonial English: varieties around the world* [14]. Cambridge University Press. ISBN 0521831407.

- Wardhaugh, Ronald (2006). *An introduction to sociolinguistics* [15]. Wiley-Blackwell. ISBN 140513559X.

External links

- Accents of English from Around the World (University of Edinburgh) [16] Hear and compare how the same 110 words are pronounced in 50 English accents from around the world – instantaneous playback online

Dictionaries

- Collection of English bilingual dictionaries [17]
- dict.org [18]
- Dictionary of American Regional English [19]
- English language word roots, prefixes and suffixes (affixes) dictionary [20]
- Oxford's online dictionary [21]
- Merriam-Webster's online dictionary [22]
- Macquarie Dictionary Online [23]

1. REDIRECT Template:Navboxes

ace:Bahsa Inggréh krc:Ингилиз тил frr:Aingelsch mhr:Англычан йылме pnb:انگریزی pcd:Inglé ckb:زمانی ئینگلیزی

Luganda

Ganda		
Luganda, Oluganda		
Spoken in	Uganda	
Region	Mainly Buganda region	
Total speakers	First language: 6 million (2008) Second language: 4 million (2008)	

Language family	Niger-Congo
	 • Atlantic-Congo
	  • Benue-Congo
	   • Bantoid
	    • Southern Bantoid
	     • Bantu
	      • Northeast Bantu
	       • Great Lakes Bantu
	        • Nyoro-Ganda
	         • Ganda	

Language codes		
ISO 639-1	lg	
ISO 639-2	lug	
ISO 639-3	lug [1]	
Linguasphere		

Ganda, or **Luganda** (Ganda: *Oluganda* [oluɡaːnda]Wikipedia:Cleanup), is the major language of Uganda, spoken by over ten million Ganda and other people mainly in Southern Uganda, including the capital Kampala. It belongs to the Bantu branch of the Niger-Congo language family. Typologically, it is a highly agglutinating language with subject-verb-object word order and nominative-accusative morphosyntactic alignment.

With about six million first-language-speakers in the Buganda region and about four million others with a working knowledge, it is the most widely spoken Ugandan language, and as second language it follows English and precedes Swahili. The language is used in some primary schools in Buganda as pupils begin to learn English, the primary official language of Uganda. Until the 1960s, Ganda was also the official language of instruction in primary schools in Eastern Uganda.

Phonology

A notable feature of Luganda phonology is its geminate consonants and distinctions between long and short vowels. Speakers generally consider consonantal gemination and vowel lengthening to be two manifestations of the same effect, which they call simply "doubling" or "stressing".

Luganda is also a tonal language; the change in the pitch of a syllable can change the meaning of a word. For example the word *kabaka* means 'king' if all three syllables are given the same pitch. If the first syllable is high then the meaning changes to 'the little one catches' (third person singular present tense Class VI *ka-* of *-baka* 'to catch'). This feature makes Luganda a difficult language for speakers of non-tonal languages to learn. A non-native speaker has to learn the variations of pitch by prolonged listening.

Vowels

	Front	Back
Close	i	u
Close-mid	e	o
Open		a

l+Luganda vowels

All five vowels have two forms: long and short. The distinction is phonemic but can occur only in certain positions. After two consonants, the latter being a semivowel, all vowels are long. Before a prenasalised consonant, all vowels are long. Before a geminate, all vowels are short. The quality of a vowel is not affected by its length.

Consonants

The table below gives the consonant set of Luganda, grouping voiceless and voiced consonants together in a cell where appropriate, in that order.

	Labial	Alveolar	Palatal	Velar
Plosive	p b	t d	c ɟ	k g
Fricative	f v [2]	s z		
Nasal	m	n	ɲ	ŋ
Approximant		l~r [1]	j	w
Trill				

1. The liquids [l] and [r] are allophones of a single phoneme /l~r/, although the distinction is reflected in the orthography.
2. The labiodental fricatives /f/ and /v/ are slightly labialised and so could also be transcribed [fʷ] and [vʷ] respectively.

Apart from /l~r/, all these consonants can be geminated, even at the start of a word: *bbiri* /bːíri/ 'two', *kitto* /cítːo/ 'cold'. The approximants /w/ and /j/ are geminated as /gːw/ and /ɟː/: *eggwanga* /egːwáːŋga/ 'country'; *jjenje* /ɟːéːɲɟe/ 'cricket'—from the roots *-wanga* /wáːŋga/ and *-yenje* /jéːɲɟe/ respectively, with the singular noun prefix *e-* that doubles the following consonant.

Apart from /l~r/, /w/ and /j/, all consonants can also be prenasalised—prefixed with a nasal consonant. This consonant will be /m/, /n/, /ɲ/ or /ŋ/ according to the place of articulation, and belongs to the same syllable as the consonant it precedes.

The liquid /l~r/ becomes /d/ when geminated or prenasalised. For example *ndaba* /ndábá/ 'I see' (from the root *-laba* with the subject prefix *n-*); *eddagala* /edːágala/ 'leaf' (from the root *-lagala* with the singular noun prefix *e-*, which doubles the following consonant.

A consonant can't be both geminated and prenasalised. When morphological processes require this, the gemination is dropped and the syllable /zi/ is inserted, which can then be prenasalised. For example when the prefix *en-* is aded to the adjective *-ddugavu* 'black' the result is *enzirugavu* /eːnzírugavu/.

The nasals /m/, /n/, /ɲ/ and /ŋ/ can be syllabic at the start of a word: *nkima* /ɲcíma/ (or [ɲtʃíma]) 'monkey', *mpa* /m̩pá/ 'I give', *nnyinyonnyola* /ɲɲiɲóɲːola/ or /ɲːiɲóɲːola/ 'I explain'. Note that this last example can be analysed in two ways, reflecting the fact that there's no distinction between prenasalisation and gemination when applied to nasal consonants.

Tone

Luganda has a simple tone system, sometimes argued to be pitch accent.

Phonotactics

Syllables can take any of the following forms:

- V (only as the first syllable of a word)
- CV
- GV
- NCV
- CSV
- GSV
- NCSV

where V = vowel, C = single consonant (including nasals and semivowels but excluding geminates), G = geminate consonant, N = nasal consonant, S = semivowel

These forms are subject to certain phonotactic restrictions:

- Two vowels may not appear adjacent to one another. When morphological or grammatical rules cause two vowels to meet, the first vowel is elided or reduced to a semivowel and the second is lengthened if possible.
- A vowel following a consonant–semivowel combination (except [gːw]) is always long. After [gːw] a vowel can be either long or short.
- A vowel followed by a nasal consonant–non-nasal consonant combination is always long.
- A vowel followed by a geminate is always short. This rule takes precedence over all the above rules.
- The velar plosives [k] and [g] may not appear before the vowel [i] or the semivowel [j]. In this position they become the corresponding postalveolar affricates [tʃ] and [dʒ] respectively.
- The consonants [j], [w] and [l]/[r] can't be geminated or prenasalised.
- A consonant can't be both geminated and prenasalised.

The net effect of this is that all Luganda words follow the general pattern of alternating consonant clusters and vowels, beginning with either but always ending in a vowel:

- (V)XVXV...XV

where V = vowel, X = consonant cluster, (V) = optional vowel

This is reflected in the syllabification rule that words are always hyphenated after a vowel (when breaking a word over two lines). For example *Emmotoka yange ezze* 'My car has arrived' would be split into syllables as *E·mmo·to·ka ya·nge e·zze*.

Variant pronunciations

The palatal plosives /c/ and /ɟ/ may be realised with some affrication—either as [cç] and [ɟʝ] or as postalveolars /tʃ/ and /dʒ/ respectively.

In speech, word-final vowels are often elided in these conditioning environments:

- Word-final /u/ can be silent after /f/, /fː/, /v/ or /vː/
- Word-final /i/ can be silent after /c/, /cː/, /ɟ/ or /ɟː/

For example, *ekiddugavu* /ecídːugavu/ 'black' may be pronounced [ecídːugavʷu] or [ecídːugavʷ]. Similarly *lwaki* /lwáːci/ 'why' may be pronounced [lwáːci], [lwáːc] or [lwáːtʃ].

Long vowels before prenasalised fricatives (that is, before /nf/, /nv/, /ns/ or /nz/) may be nasalised. Additionally the /n/ usually becomes a labiodental in /nf/, /nv/. For example:

- *nfa* /fa/ 'I'm dying' is pronounced [ɱfʷa]
- *musanvu* /musáːnvu/ 'seven' may be pronounced [musáːɱvʷu], [musãːɱvʷu], [musãːvʷu] or [musãːɱvʷ]
- *tonsabe* /toːnsábe/ 'don't ask me' may be pronounced [toːnsábe], [tõːsábe] or [tõːnsábe]

The liquid /l~r/ has two allophones [l] and [r], conditioned by the preceding vowel. It's usually realised as a tap or flap [r] after a close unrounded vowel (*i.e.* after /e/, /eː/, /i/ or /iː/), and as a lateral approximant [l] elsewhere. However, there's considerable variation in this.

Alternative analysis

Treating the geminate and prenasalised consonants as separate phonemes yields the expanded consonant set below:

	Labial	Alveolar	Palatal	Velar
Simple plosive	p b	t d	c ɟ	k g
Geminate plosive	pː bː	tː dː	cː ɟː	kː gː
Prenasalised plosive	mp mb	nt nd	ɲc ɲɟ	ŋk ŋg
Simple fricative	f v	s z		
Geminate fricative	fː vː	sː zː		
Prenasalised fricative	mɸ mv	ns nz		
Simple nasal	m	n	ɲ	ŋ
Geminate nasal	mː	nː	ɲː	ŋː
Approximant			j	w
Liquid		l		

This simplifies the phonotactic rules so that all syllables are of one of three forms:

- V (only as the first syllable of a word)
- CV
- CSV

where V = vowel, C = consonant (including geminate and prenasalised consonants), N = nasal consonant, S = semivowel (*i.e.* either /j/ or /w/).

Vowel length is then only distinctive before simple consonants (*i.e.* simple plosives, simple fricatives, simple nasals, approximants and liquids).

Orthography

Luganda spelling, which has been standardised since 1947, uses the Roman alphabet augmented with one new letter *ŋ* and a digraph *ny* which is treated as a single letter. It has a very high sound-to-letter correspondence: one letter usually represents one sound and vice-versa.

The distinction between simple and geminate consonants is always represented explicitly: simple consonants are written single; geminates are written double. The distinction between long and short vowels is always made clear from the spelling, but not always explicitly: short vowels are always written single; long vowels are only written double when their length cannot be inferred from the context. Stress and tones are not represented in the spelling.

The following phonemes are always represented with the same letter or combination of letters:

- Short vowels (always spelt *a, e, i, o, u*)
- All consonants apart from /l~r/, /c/ and /ɟ/
- The palatals /c/ and /ɟ/, when followed by a short vowel (always spelt *c, j*), except when the short vowel is itself followed by a geminate consonant, or when the vowel is /i/

The following phonemes can be represented with two letters or combinations of letters, with the alternation predictable from the context:

- Long vowels (spelt *a, e, i, o, u* where short vowels are impossible; *aa, ee, ii, oo, uu* elsewhere)
- The liquid /l~r/ (spelt *r* after *e* or *i*; *l* elsewhere)

The following phonemes can be represented with two letters or combinations of letters, with unpredictable alternation between the two:

- The palatals /c/ and /ɟ/, when followed by a long vowel, by a short vowel and a geminate consonant, or by an *i* sound (/i/ or /i:/) (can be spelt with *c, j*, with *ky, gy*, or, before *i*, with *k, g*)

It is therefore possible to predict the pronunciation of any word (with the exception of stress and tones) from the spelling. It's also usually possible to predict the spelling of a word from the pronunciation. The only words where this is not possible are those that include one of the affricate–vowel combinations discussed above.

Vowels

The five vowels in Luganda are spelt with the same letters as in many other languages (for example Spanish):

- *a* /a/
- *e* /e/
- *i* /i/
- *o* /o/
- *u* /u/

As mentioned above, the distinction between long and short vowels is phonemic and is therefore represented in the orthography. Long vowels are written as double (when length cannot be inferred from the context) and short vowels are written single. For example:

- *bana* /bana/ 'four (*e.g.* people)' vs *baana* /baːna/ 'children'
- *sera* /sela/ 'dance' vs *seera* /seːla/ 'overcharge'
- *sira* /sila/ 'mingle' vs *siira* /siːla/ 'walk slowly'
- *kola* /kola/ 'do' vs *koola* /koːla/ '(to) weed'
- *tuma* /tuma/ 'send' vs *tuuma* /tuːma/ '(to) name'

In certain contexts, phonotactic constraints mean that a vowel must be long, and in these cases it is not written double:

- A vowel followed by a prenasalised consonant
- A vowel that comes after a consonant–semivowel combination—apart from *ggw* which can be thought of as a geminated *w*, and *ggy* which can be thought of as a geminated *y* (although the latter is less common as this combination is more often spelt *jj*)

For example:

- *ekyuma* /ecúːma/ 'metal'
- *ŋŋenda* /ŋŋéːnda/ 'I go'

But

- *eggwolezo* /egːwólezo/ 'court house'
- *eggwoolezo* /egːwóːlezo/ 'customs office'

Vowels at the start or end of the word are not written double, even if they are long. The only exception to this (apart from all-vowel interjections such as *eee* and *uu*) is *yee* 'yes'.

Consonants

With the exception of *ny* [ɲ], each consonant sound in Luganda corresponds to a single letter. The *ny* combination is treated as a single letter and therefore doesn't have any effect on vowel length (see the previous subsection).

The following letters are pronounced as in English:

- *b* /b/
- *d* /d/
- *f* /f/
- *l* /l/
- *m* /m/
- *n* /n/
- *p* /p/
- *s* /s/

- *t* /t/
- *v* /v/
- *w* /w/
- *y* /j/
- *z* /z/

A few letters have unusual values:

- *c* /c/
- *j* /ɟ/
- *ny* /ɲ/
- *ŋ* /ŋ/

The letters *l* and *r* represent the same sound in Luganda—[l]—but the orthography requires *r* after *e* or *i*, and *l* elsewhere:

- *alinda* /alíːnda/ 'she's waiting'
- *akirinda* /acilíːnda/ (or [aciríːnda]) 'she's waiting for it'

There are also two letters whose pronunciation depends on the following letter:

- *k* is pronounced /c/ (or /tʃ/) before *i* or *y*, /k/ elsewhere
- *g* is pronounced /ɟ/ (or /dʒ/) before *i* or *y*, /g/ elsewhere

Compare this to the pronunciation of *c* and *g* in many Romance languages. As in the Romance languages the 'softening letter' (in Italian *i*; in French *e*; in Luganda *y*) is not itself pronounced, although in Luganda it does have the effect of lengthening the following vowel (see the previous subsection).

Finally the sounds /ɲ/ and /ŋ/ are spelt *n* before another consonant with the same place of articulation (in other words, before other palatals and velars respectively) rather than *ny* and *ŋ*:

- The combinations /ɲɲ/ and /ɲː/ are spelt *nny*
- The combination /ɲj/ is spelt *nÿ* (the diaeresis shows that the *y* is a separate letter rather than part of the *ny* digraph, and the /ɲ/ is spelt *n* before *y* as in the above rule; in practice this combination is very rare)
- /ŋ/ is spelt *n* before *k* or *g* (but not before another *ŋ*)
- /ɲ/ is spelt *n* before *c* or *j*, or before a soft *k* or *g*

Alphabet

The standard Luganda alphabet is composed of twenty-four letters:

```
* 18 consonants: b, p, v, f, m, d, t, l, r, n, z, s, j, c, g, k, ŋ, ny
* 5 vowels: a, e, i, o, u
* 2 semi-vowels: w, y
```

Since the last consonant ŋ does not appear on standard typewriters or computer keyboards, it is often replaced by the combination *ng'*—including the apostrophe. In some non-standard orthographies, the apostrophe is not used, which can lead to confusion with the letter combination *ng*, which is different from ŋ.

In addition, the letter combination *ny* is treated as a unique consonant. When the letters *n* and *y* appear next to each other, they are written as *nÿ*, with the diaeresis mark to distinguish this combination from *ny*.

Other letters (*h, q, x*) are not used in the standard orthography, but are often used to write loanwords from other languages. Most such loanwords have standardised spellings consistent with Luganda orthography (and therefore not using these letters), but these spelling are not often used, particularly for English words.

The full alphabet, including both standard Luganda letters and those used only for loanwords, is as follows:

- Aa, *a*
- Bb, *bba*
- Cc, *cca*
- Dd, *dda*
- Ee, *e*
- Ff, *ffa*
- Gg, *gga*
- (Hh, *ha* [1])
- Ii, *yi*
- Jj, *jja*
- Kk, *kka*
- Ll, *la*
- Mm, *mma*
- Nn, *nna*
- (NY Ny ny, *nnya* or *nna-ya*) [2]
- Ŋŋ, *ŋŋa*
- Oo, *o*
- Pp, *ppa*
- (Qq [1])
- Rr, *eri*
- Ss, *ssa*
- Tt, *tta*
- Uu, *wu*
- Vv, *vva*

- Ww, *wa*
- (Xx [1])
- Yy, *ya*
- Zz, *zza*

1. The letters *h*, *q* and *x* are included when reciting the alphabet and are usually given their English names (apart from *ha*).
2. The digraph *ny*, although considered a separate letter for orthographic purposes, is generally treated as a combination of *n* and *y* for other purposes. It's not included when reciting the alphabet.

Grammar

Like the grammars of most Bantu languages, Luganda's grammar can be said to be *noun-centric* in the sense that most words in a sentence agree with a noun. Agreement is by gender and number, and is indicated with prefixes and infixes attached to the start of word stems. The following parts of speech agree with nouns in class and number:

- adjective
- verb (for subject and object roles)
- pronoun
- possessive

Noun classes

NB: In the study of Bantu languages the term *noun class* is often used to refer to what is called gender in comparative linguistics and in the study of certain other languages. Hereafter, both terms may be used.

There is some disagreement as to how to count Luganda's noun classes. Some authorities count singular and plural forms as two separate noun classes while others treat the singular–plural pairs as genders. By the former method there are 17 classes while by the latter there are 10, since there are two pairs of classes with identical plurals and one class with no singular–plural distinction.

The latter method is consistent with the study of non-Bantu languages: it is recognised, for example, that German has three genders—masculine, feminine and neuter—and two numbers—singular and plural. To ignore the grammatical and semantic relationship between 'masculine singular' and 'masculine plural' (for example *Mann* 'man' and *Männer* 'men') and to treat them as two different noun classes out of a total of six would be artificial; so number is regarded as being distinct from gender, giving three genders and two numbers. Applying this method to Luganda gives ten noun classes, nine of which have separate singular and plural forms. This is the usual way to discuss Luganda (but not when discussing Bantu languages generally).

The following table shows how the ten traditional classes of Luganda map onto the Proto-Bantu noun classes:

Luganda Class	Number	Proto-Bantu Class
I	Singular	1, 1a
	Plural	2
II	Singular	3
	Plural	4
III	Singular	9
	Plural	10
IV	Singular	7
	Plural	8
V	Singular	5
	Plural	6
VI	Singular	12
	Plural	14
VII	Singular	11
	Plural	10
VIII	Singular	20
	Plural	22
IX	Singular	15
	Plural	6
X	(no distinction)	13

As the table shows, Proto-Bantu's polyplural classes (6 and 10) are treated as separate in this article.

As is the case with most languages, the distribution of nouns among the classes is essentially arbitrary, but there are some loose patterns:

- Class I contains mainly people, although some inanimate nouns can be found in this class: *musajja* 'man', *kaawa* 'coffee'
- Class II contains all sorts of nouns but most of the concrete nouns in Class II are long or cylindrical. Most trees fall into this class: *muti* 'tree'
- Class III also contains many different types of concepts but most animals fall into this class: *mbwa* 'dog'
- Class IV contains inanimate objects and is the class used for the impersonal 'it': *ekitabo* 'book'

- Class V contains mainly (but not exclusively) large things and liquids, and can also be used to create augmentatives: *ebbeere* 'breast', *lintu* 'giant' (from *muntu* 'person')
- Class VI contains mainly small things and can be used to create diminutives, adjectival abstract nouns and (in the plural) negative verbal nouns and countries: *kabwa* 'puppy' (from *mbwa* 'dog'), *kanafu* 'laziness' (from *munafu* 'lazy'), *bukola* 'inaction, not to do' (from *kukola* 'to do, act'), *Bungereza* 'Britain, England' (from *Mungereza* 'British, English person')
- Class VII contains many different things including the names of most languages: *Oluganda* 'Luganda', *Oluzungu* 'English language' (from *muzungu* 'European, white person*)
- Class VIII is rarely used but can be used to create pejorative forms: *gubwa* 'mutt' (from *mbwa* 'dog')
- Class IX is mainly used for infinitives or affirmative verbal nouns: *kukola* 'action, to do' (from the verb *kola* 'do, act')
- Class X, which has no singular–plural distinction, is used for mass nouns, usually in the sense of 'a drop' or 'precious little': *tuzzi* 'drop of water' (from *mazzi* 'water'), *tubaka* 'sleep'

The class that a noun belongs to can usually be determined by its prefix:

- Class I: singular *(o)mu-*, plural *(a)ba-*
- Class II: singular *(o)mu-*, plural *(e)mi-*
- Class III: singular *(e)n-*, plural *(e)n-*
- Class IV: singular *(e)ki-*, plural *(e)bi-*
- Class V: singular *li-*, *eri-*, plural *(a)ma-*
- Class VI: singular *(a)ka-*, plural *(o)bu-*
- Class VII: singular *(o)lu-*, plural *(e)n-*
- Class VIII: singular *(o)gu-*, plural *(a)ga-*
- Class IX: singular *(o)ku-*, plural *(a)ma-*
- Class X: *(o)tu-*

There are a few only cases where prefixes overlap: the singulars of Classes I and II (both beginning with *mu-*); the singular of Class III and plurals of Classes III and VII (all beginning with *n-*); and the plurals of Classes V and IX (both *ma-*). Genuine ambiguity, however, is rare, since even where the noun prefixes are the same, the other prefixes are often different. For example there can be no confusion between *omuntu* (Class I) 'person' and *omuntu* (Class II) 'seat' in the sentences *Omuntu ali wano* 'The person is here' and *Omuntu guli wano* 'The seat is here' because the verb prefixes *a-* (Class I) and *gu-* (Class II) are different, even if the noun prefixes are the same. The same is true with the singular and plural of Class III: *Embwa erya* 'The dog is eating' vs *Embwa zirya* 'The dogs are eating' (compare English *The sheep is eating* vs *The sheep are eating* where the noun is invariant but the verb distinguishes singular from plural).

In fact, the plurals of Classes III and VII, and those of Classes V and IX, are identical in all their prefixes (noun, verb, adjective *etc.*).

Class V uses its noun prefixes a little differently from the other classes. The singular noun prefix, *eri-*, is often reduced to *e-* with an accompanying doubling of the stem's initial consonant. This happens when the stem begins with a single non-nasal consonant, or a single nasal consonant followed by a long vowel, a nasal consonant and then a non-nasal consonant (called a *nasalised stem*). For example:

* *eggi* 'egg'; plural *amagi* (from stem *gi*)
* *eggwanga* 'country'; plural *amawanga* (from nasalised stem *wanga*—the *w* becomes *ggw* when doubled)
* *ejjinja* 'cricket'; plural *amayinja* (from nasalised stem *yinja*—the *y* becomes *jj* when doubled)

Other stems use the full prefix:

* *erinnya* 'name'; plural *amannya* (from stem *nnya*)
* *eriiso* 'eye'; plural *amaaso* (from stem *yiso*)
* *eryanda* 'battery'; plural *amanda* (from stem *anda*)

There are also some nouns that have no prefix. Their genders must simply be learnt by rote:

* Class I: *ssebo* 'gentleman, sir', *nnyabo* 'madam', *Katonda* 'god', *kabaka* 'king', *kyayi* (or *caayi*) 'tea', *kaawa* 'coffee'
* Class III: *kkapa* 'cat', *gomesi* 'gomesi (traditional East African women's formal dress)'

Adjectives, verbs, certain adverbs, the possessive and a few special forms of conjunctions are inflected to agree with nouns in Luganda.

Nouns

Nouns are inflected for number and state.

Number is indicated by replacing the singular prefix with the plural prefix. For example *omusajja* 'man', *abasajja* 'men'; *ekisanirizo* 'comb ebisanirizo 'combs'. All word classes agree with nouns in number and class.

State is similar to case but applies to verbs and other parts of speech as well as nouns, pronouns and adjectives. There are two states in Luganda, which may be called the base state and the topic state. The base state is unmarked and the topic state is indicated by the presence of the initial vowel.

The topic state is used for nouns in the following conditions:

* Subject of a sentence
* Object of an affirmative verb (other than the verb 'to be')

The base state is used for the following conditions:

* Object of a negative verb
* Object of a preposition
* Noun predicate (whether or not there's an explicit copula or verb 'to be')

Adjectives

As in other Niger-Congo languages (as well as most Indo-European and Afro-Asiatic languages), adjectives must agree in gender and number with the noun they qualify. For example:

- *omuwala omulungi* 'beautiful girl' (Class I, singular)
- *abawala abalungi* 'beautiful girls' (Class I, plural)
- *emmotoka ennungi* 'beautiful/good car' (Class V, singular)
- *amamotoka amalungi* 'beautiful/good cars' (Class V, plural)

The adjective *-lungi* changes its prefix according to the gender (Class I or II) and number (singular or plural) or the noun it's qualifying (compare Italian *bella ragazza, belle ragazze, bel ragazzo, belli ragazzi*).

Attributive adjectives agree in state with the noun they qualify, but predicative adjectives never take the initial vowel. Similarly, the subject relative is formed by adding the initial vowel to the verb (because a main verb is a predicate.

Verbs

As in other Bantu languages, every verb must also agree with its subject in gender and number (as opposed to number only as in Indo-European languages). For example:

- *omusajja anywa* 'the man is drinking' (Class I, singular)
- *abasajja banywa* 'the men are drinking' (Class I, plural)
- *embuzi enywa* 'the goat is drinking' (Class III, singular)
- *embuzi zinywa* 'the goats are drinking' (Class III, plural)
- *akaana kanywa* 'the baby/infant is drinking' (Class VI, singular)
- *obwana bunywa* 'the babies/infants are drinking' (Class VI, plural)

Here, the verb *nywa* changes its prefix according to the gender and number of its subject (compare Arabic number and gender agreement in a topicalized-subject construction: *ar-rajul yashrib* 'the man drinks', *ar-rijaal yashribou* 'the men drink', *al-mara'ah tashrib* 'the woman drinks', *an-nisaa' yashribna* 'the women drink').

Note, in the second and third examples, how the verb agrees with the number of the noun even when the noun doesn't explicitly reflect the number distinction.

When the verb governs one or more objects, there is an agreement between the object infixes and the gender and number of their antecedents:

- *mmunywa* 'I drink it (*e.g.* coffee)' (*kaawa* 'coffee', Class I singular)
- *nganywa* 'I drink it (*e.g.* water)' (*amazzi* 'water', Class IX plural)

See also the detailed section on verbs below.

Adverbs

True adverbs in the grammatical sense are far rarer in Luganda than in, say, English, being mostly translated by other parts of speech—for example adjectives or particles. When the adverb is qualifying a verb, it's usually translated by an adjective, which then agrees with the subject of the verb. For example:

- *Ankonjera bubi* 'She slanders me badly'
- *Bankonjera bubi* 'They slander me badly'

Here, 'badly' is translated with the adjective *-bi* 'bad, ugly', which is declined to agree with the subject.

Other concepts can be translated by invariant particles. for example the intensifying particle *nnyo* is attached to an adjective or verb to mean 'very', 'a lot'. For example: *Lukwago anywa nnyo* 'Lukwago drinks a lot'.

There are also two groups of true adverb in Luganda, both of which agree with the verbal subject or qualified noun (not just in gender and number but also in person), but which are inflected differently. The first group is conjugated in the same way as verbs and contains only a few words: *tya* 'how', *ti* 'like this', *tyo* 'like that':

- *Njogera bwe nti* 'I speak like this'
- *Abasiraamu basaba bwebati* 'Muslims pray like this'
- *Enkima erya bweti* 'The monkey eats like this'
- *Enkima zirya bweziti* 'Monkeys eat like this'

The adverb *ti* 'like this' (the last word in each of the above sentences) is conjugated as a verb to agree with the subject of the sentence in gender, number and person.

The second group takes a different set of prefixes, based on the pronouns. Adverbs in this group inclusde *-nna* 'all' (or, with the singular, 'any'), *-kka* 'only', *-mbi, -mbiriri* 'both' and *-nsatule* 'all three':

- *Nkola nzekka* 'I work alone'
- *Nzekka nze nkola* 'Only I work'
- *Ggwe wekka ggwe okola* 'Only you work'
- *Nze nzekka nze ndigula emmotoka* 'Only I will buy the car'
- *Ndigula mmotoka yokka* 'I will only buy the car'

Note how, in the last two examples, the adverb *-kka* agrees with whichever antecedent it's qualifying—either the implicit *nze* 'I' or the explicit *emmotoka* 'the car'.

Note also, in the first two examples, how the placement of *nzekka* before or after the verb makes the difference between 'only' (when the adverb qualifies and agrees with the subject—the implicit *nze* 'I') and 'alone' (when it qualifies the verb *nkola* 'I work' but agrees with the subject).

Possessive

The possessive in Luganda is indicated with a different particle for each singular and plural noun class (according to the possessed noun). An alternative way of thinking about the Luganda possessive is as a single word whose initial consonant cluster is altered to agree with the possessed noun in class and number.

Depending on the possessed noun, the possessive takes one of the following forms:

- Singular *wa*, plural *ba* (Class I)
- Singular *gwa*, plural *gya* (Class II)
- Singular *ya*, plural *za* (Class III)
- Singular *kya*, plural *bya* (Class IV)
- Singular *lya*, plural *ga* (Class V)
- Singular *ka*, plural *bwa* (Class VI)
- Singular *lwa*, plural *za* (Class VII)
- Singular *gwa*, plural *ga* (Class VIII)
- Singular *kwa*, plural *ga* (Class IX)
- *Twa* (Class X)

If the possessor is a personal pronoun, the separate possessive form is not used. Instead, the following personal possessives are used:

- *Wange* 'my', *wo* 'your (singular possessor)', *we* 'his, her'; *waffe* 'our', *wammwe* 'your (plural possessor)', *waabwe* 'their' (Class I, singular possessed noun)
- *Bange* 'my', *bo* 'your (singular possessor)', *be* 'his, her'; *baffe* 'our', *bammwe* 'your (plural possessor)', *baabwe* 'their' (Class I, plural possessed noun)
- *Gwange* 'my', *gwo* 'your (singular possessor)', *gwe* 'his, her'; *gwaffe* 'our', *gwammwe* 'your (plural possessor)', *gwabwe* 'their' (Class II, singular possessed noun)
- *Gyange* 'my', *gyo* 'your (singular possessor)', *gye* 'his, her'; *gyaffe* 'our', *gyammwe* 'your (plural possessor)' *gyabwe* 'their' (Class II, plural possessed noun)
- *Yange* 'my', *yo* 'your', *etc.* (Class III, singular possessed noun)
- *Etc.*

Compare these to the French possessive adjectives:

- *Mon* 'my', *ton* 'your (singular possessor)', *son* 'his, her, its'; *notre* 'our', *votre* 'your (plural possessor)', *leur* 'their'—Masculine singular possessed noun
- *Ma* 'my', *ta* 'your (singular possessor)', *sa* 'his, her, its'; *notre* 'our', *votre* 'your (plural possessor)', *leur* 'their'—Masculine singular possessed noun
- *Mes* 'my', *tes* 'your (singular possessor)', *ses* 'his, her, its'; *nos* 'our', *vos* 'your (plural possessor)', *leurs* 'their'—Plural possessed noun

There are also a few nouns that take special forms when used with a possessive:

- *Kitange* 'my father', *kitaawo* 'your (singular) father', *kitaawe* 'his/her father'

Verbs

Luganda verbs are inflected for person, number, tense, mood and the gender of the subject and, if present, objects.

Subject and objects

The subject of a verb is indicated with a prefix that agrees with the antecedent in person and number. In the third person the prefix also agrees in noun class with its antecedent.

The subject prefixes for the personal pronouns are:

- First person: singular *n-* 'I', plural *tu-* 'we'
- Second person: singular *o-* 'you (singular)', *mu-* 'you (plural)'
- Third person: singular *a-* 'he, she', *ba-* 'they (Class I)'

For impersonal pronouns the subject prefixes are:

- Class I: singular *a-*, plural *ba-* (*i.e.* the third person prefixes shown directly above)
- Class II: singular *gu-*, plural *gi-*
- Class III: singular *e-*, plural *zi-*
- Class IV: singular *ki-*, plural *bi-*
- Class V: singular *li-*, plural *ga-*
- Class VI: singular *ka-*, plural *bu-*
- Class VII: singular *lu-*, plural *zi-*
- Class VIII: singular *gu-*, plural *ga-*
- Class IX: singular *ku-*, plural *ga-*
- Class X: *tu-*

When a verb governs one or more objects, they are shown with infixes that agree with the antecedent in person and number. As with the subject prefix, the third person infixes also agree with their antecedents in noun class. The personal object infixes are:

- First person: singular *-n-* 'me', plural *-tu-* 'us'
- Second person: singular *-ku-* 'you (singular)', *-ba-* 'you (plural)'
- Third person: singular *-mu-* 'him, her', *-ba-* 'them (Class I)'

For the third person the object prefixes are:

- Class I: singular *-mu-*, plural *-ba-* (*i.e.* the third person prefixes shown directly above)
- Class II: singular *-gu-*, plural *-gi-*
- Class III: singular *-ta-*, plural *-zi-*
- Class IV: singular *-ki-*, plural *-bi-*
- Class V: singular *-li-*, plural *-ga-*

- Class VI: singular *-ka-*, plural *-bu-*
- Class VII: singular *-lu-*, plural *-zi-*
- Class VIII: singular *-gu-*, plural *-ga-*
- Class IX: singular *-ku-*, plural *-ga-*
- Class X: *-tu-*

Note the similarity between each subject prefix and the corresponding object infix: they are the same in all cases except Class I and the singular of Class III. Note also the correspondence between the object infixes and the noun prefixes (see Nouns above): when every *m-* in the noun prefix is replaced by a *g-* in the object infix, the only differences are in Classes I and III.

The direct object infix is usually inserted directly after the subject prefix:

- *nkiridde* 'I have eaten it' (*n-* subject 'I' + *-ki-* object 'it' + *-ridde* verb 'ate')

The indirect object infix comes after the direct object:

- *nkimuwadde* 'I have given it to him' (*n-* subject 'I' + *-ki-* object 'it' + *-mu-* object '(to) him' + *-wadde* verb 'gave')

Negative

The negative is usually formed by prefixing *te-* or *t-* to the subject prefix, or, in the case of the first person singular, replacing the prefix with *si-*. This results in the following set of personal subject prefixes:

- First person: singular *si-* 'I', plural *tetu-* 'we'
- Second person: singular *to-* 'you (singular)', *temu-* 'you (plural)'
- Third person: singular *ta-* 'he, she', *teba-* 'they (Class I)'

The negative impersonal subject prefixes are:

- Class I: singular *ta-*, plural *teba-* (*i.e.* the third person prefixes shown directly above)
- Class II: singular *tegu-*, plural *tegi-*
- Class III: singular *te-*, plural *tezi-*
- Class IV: singular *teki-*, plural *tebi-*
- Class V: singular *teri-*, plural *tega-*
- Class VI: singular *teka-*, plural *tebu-*
- Class VII: singular *telu-*, plural *tezi-*
- Class VIII: singular *tegu-*, plural *tega-*
- Class IX: singular *teku-*, plural *tega-*
- Class X: *tetu-*

When used with object relatives or the narrative tense (see below), the negative is formed with the infix *-ta-*, which is inserted after the subject and object affixes:

- *Omuntu gwe nnalabye* 'The person whom I saw'

- *Omuntu gwe ssalabye* 'The person whom I didn't see'

Modified stem

To form some tenses, a special form of the verb stem, called the 'modified form', is used. This is formed by making various changes to the final syllable of the stem, usually involving either changing the final syllable to one of the following suffixes:

- *-se*
- *-sse*
- *-ze*
- *-zze*
- *-izze*
- *-ezze*
- *-nye*
- *-nyi*
- *-ye*
- *-de*
- *-dde*

The modified form of verb stems is the only real source of irregularity in Luganda's verbal system. Monosyllabic verbs, in particular, have unpredictable modified forms:

- *okuba* 'to be' *-badde*
- *okufa* 'to die' *-fudde*
- *okugaana* 'to deny, forbid' *-gaanyi*
- *okuggwa* 'to end' (intransitive) *-wedde*
- *okuggya* 'to remove' *-ggye* or *-ggyidde*
- *okuggya* 'to cook' (intransitive) *-yidde*
- *okugwa* 'to fall' *-gudde*
- *okujja* 'to come' *-zze*
- *okukka* 'to go down, come down' *-sse*
- *okukwata* 'to catch' *-kutte*
- *okulwa* 'to delay' *-ludde*
- *okulya* 'to eat' *-lidde*
- *okumanyi* 'to find out, realise' *-manyi*
- *okunywa* 'to drink' *-nywedde*
- *okuta* 'to release' *-tadde*
- *okuteeka* 'to put' *-tadde*
- *okutta* 'to kill' *-sse*
- *okutwaka* 'to take' *-tutte*

- *okutya* 'to be afraid' *-tidde*
- *okuva* 'to come from' *-vudde*
- *okuwa* 'to give' *-wadde*
- *okuyita* 'to call' *-yise*
- *okuyita* 'to pass' *-yise*

Tense

Tense in Luganda is explicitly marked on the verb, as it is in most other Bantu languages.

Present tense

The present tense is formed by simply adding the subject prefixes to the stem. The negative is formed in the same way but with the negative subject prefixes (this is the usual way of forming the negative in Luganda).

Inflection	Gloss	Negative	Gloss
nkola	'I do'	*sikola*	'I don't do'
okola	'you do'	*tokola*	'you don't do'
akola	'he, she does'	*takola*	'he, she doesn't do'
tukola	'we do'	*tetukola*	'we don't do'
mukola	'you (plural) do'	*temukola*	'you (plural) don't do'
bakola	'they (class I) do'	*tebakola*	'they (class I) don't do'
gukola	'it (class II) does'	*tegukola*	'it (class II) doesn't do'
bikola	'they (class IV) do'	*tebikola*	'they (class IV) don't do'
zikola	'they (class VII) do'	*tezikola*	'they (class VII) don't do'

I+Examples of present tense inflection

The present perfect is just the subject prefix plus the modified stem:

- *nkoze* 'I have done'
- *okoze* 'you have done'
- *akoze* 'he, she has done'
- *tukoze* 'we have done'
- *mukoze* 'you (plural) have done'
- *bakoze* 'they (class I) have done'

The present perfect in Luganda is sometimes slightly weaker in its past meaning than in English. It's often used with intransitive verbs with the sense of being in the state of having done something. For example *baze azze* means 'my husband has arrived' (using the present perfect form *-zze* of the verb *jja* 'to come'; *ŋŋenze* usually means 'I'm off' rather than 'I have gone'. But to say *I have done* in Muganda would usually use one of the past tenses *nnakoze* or *nnakola* 'I did' because *kola* is a transitive verb.

The present perfect is also used to show physical attitude. For example, using the verb *okutuula* 'to sit down': *ntuula* (present tense) means 'I am in the process of sitting myself down'; to say 'I'm sitting down' in the usual English sense of 'I'm seated', a Muganda would use the present perfect: *ntudde*.

Past tenses

The near past is formed by inserting the infix *-a-* before the modified form of the stem. This infix, being a vowel, has the effect of changing the form of the subject prefixes:

- *nnakoze* 'I did'
- *wakoze* 'you did'
- *yakoze* 'he, she did'
- *twakoze* 'we did'
- *mwakoze* 'you (plural) did'
- *baakoze* 'they (class I) did'
- ...

The near past tense is used for events that have happened in the past 18 hours. The negative is formed in the usual way.

The far past is formed with the same infix *-a-* as the near past, but using the simple form of the stem:

- *nnakola* 'I did'
- *wakola* 'you did'
- *yakola* 'he, she did'
- *twakola* 'we did'
- *mwakola* 'you (plural) did'
- *baakola* 'they (class I) did'
- ...

The far past tense is used for events that happened more than 18 hours ago, and can also be used as a weak pluperfect. This is the tense that's used in novels and storytelling.

Future tenses

The near future is used when describing things that are going to happen within the next 18 hours. It's formed with the infix -*naa-* on the simple form of the stem:

- *nnaakola* 'I shall do'
- *onookola* 'you will do'
- *anaakola* 'he, she will do'
- *tunaakola* 'we shall do'
- *munaakola* 'you (plural) will do'
- *banaakola* 'they (class I) will do'
- *eneekola* 'they (class III) will do'
- *zinaakola* 'they (class III) will do'
- ...

In the second person singular and the singular of Class III, the infix becomes -*noo-* and -*nee-* in harmony with the subject prefix.

The negative form of this tense is formed by changing the final -*a* of the stem to an -*e* and using vowel-lengthened negative subject prefixes; no tense infix is used:

- *siikole* 'I shan't do'
- *tookole* 'you won't do'
- *taakole* 'he, she won't do'
- *tetuukole* 'we shan't do'
- *temuukole* 'you (plural) won't do'
- *tebaakole* 'they (class I) won't do'
- *teguukole* 'it (class II) won't do'
- *tegiikole* 'they (class II) won't do'
- *teekole* 'he, she, it (class III) won't do'
- *teziikole* 'they (class III) won't do'
- ...

The far future is used for events that will take place more than 18 hours in the future. It's formed with the infix -*li-* on the simple form of the stem:

- *ndikola* 'I shall do'
- *olikola* 'you will do'
- *alikola* 'he, she will do'
- *tulikola* 'we shall do'
- *mulikola* 'you (plural) will do'
- *balikola* 'they (class I) will do'
- ...

Note how the *l* of the tense infix becomes a *d* after the *n-* of the first person singular subject prefix.

Other tenses

The conditional mood is formed with the infix *-andi-* and the modified form of the stem:

- *nnandikoze* 'I would do'
- *wandikoze* 'you would do'
- *yandikoze* 'he, she would do'
- *twandikoze* 'we would do'
- *mwandikoze* 'you (plural) would do'
- *bandikoze* 'they (class I) would do'

The subjunctive is a tense in Luganda, rather than a mood as in some languages. It's formed by changing the final *-a* of the stem to an *-e*:

- *nkole* 'I may do'
- *okole* 'you may do'
- *akole* 'he, she may do'
- *tukole* 'we may do'
- *mukole* 'you may do'
- *bakole* 'they may do'

The negative is formed either with the auxiliary verb *lema* ('to fail') plus the infinitive:

- *nneme kukola* 'I may not do'
- *oleme kukola* 'you may not do'
- *aleme kukola* 'he, she may not do'
- *tuleme kukola* 'we may not do'
- *muleme kukola* 'you may not do'
- *baleme kukola* 'they may not do'

or using the same forms as the negative of the near future:

- *siikole* 'I may not do'
- *tookole* 'you may not do'
- *taakole* 'he, she may not do'
- *tetuukole* 'we may not do'
- *temuukole* 'you may not do'
- *tebaakole* 'they may not do'

Luganda has some special tenses not found in many other languages. The 'still' tense is used to say that something is still happening. It's formed with the infix *-kya-*:

- *nkyakola* 'I'm still doing'
- *okyakola* 'you're still doing'

- *akyakola* 'he, she is still doing'
- *tukyakola* 'we're still doing'
- *mukyakola* 'you're still doing'
- *bakyakola* 'they're still doing'

In the negative it means 'no longer':

- *sikyakola* 'I'm no longer doing'
- *tokyakola* 'you're no longer doing'
- *takyakola* 'he, she is no longer doing'
- *tetukyakola* 'we're no longer doing'
- *temukyakola* 'you're no longer doing'
- *tebakyakola* 'they're no longer doing'

With intransitive verbs, especially verbs of physical attitude (see Present Perfect above), the *-kya-* infix can also be used with the modified verb stem to give a sense of 'still being in a state'. For example *nkyatudde* means 'I'm still seated'.

The 'so far' tense is used when talking about what has happened so far, with the implication that more is to come. It's formed with the infix *-aaka-*:

- *nnaakakola* 'I have so far done'
- *waakakola* 'you have so far done'
- *yaakakola* 'he, she has so far done'
- *twaakakola* 'we have so far done'
- *mwaakakola* 'you have so far done'
- *baakakola* 'they have so far done'

This tense is found only in the affirmative. The 'not yet' tense, on the other hand, is found only in the negative. It's used to talk about things that haven't happened yet (but which may well happen in the future), and is formed with the infix *-nna-*:

- *sinnakola* 'I haven't yet done'
- *tonnakola* 'you haven't yet done'
- *tannakola* 'he, she hasn't yet done'
- *tetunnakola* 'we haven't yet done'
- *temunnakola* 'you haven't yet done'
- *bannakola* 'they haven't yet done'

When describing a series of events that happen (or will or did happen) sequentially, the narrative form is used for all but the first verb in the sentence. It's formed by the particle *ne* (or *n'* before a vowel) followed by the present tense:

- *Nnagenda ne nkuba essimu* 'I went and made a phone call'
- *Ndigenda ne nkuba essimu* 'I'll go and make a phone call'

The narrative can be used with any tense, as long as the events it describes are in immediate sequence. The negative is formed with the infix -*si*- placed immediately after the object infixes (or after the subject prefix if no object infixes are used):

- *Saagenda era ssaakuba ssimu* 'I didn't go and did not make a phone call'
- *Sirigenda era ssirikuba ssimu* 'I won't go and will not make a phone call'
- *Ssigenze era ssikubye* 'I haven't gone to make it yet'

Compare this with the negative construction used with the object relatives.

Auxiliary verbs

Other tenses can be formed periphrastically, with the use of auxiliary verbs. Some of Luganda's auxiliary verbs can also be used as main verbs; some are always auxiliaries:

- *okuba* 'to be': used with an optional *nga* with another finite verb to form compound tenses
- *okujja* 'to come': forms a future tense when used with the infinitive of the main verb
- *okulyoka* or *okulyokka* (only used as an auxiliary): appears with another finite verb, usually translated 'and then' or (in the subjunctive) 'so that'
- *okumala* 'to finish': used with the infinitive to denote completed action, or with the stem of the main verb prefixed with *ga*- to mean 'whether one wants to or not'
- *okutera* (only used as an auxiliary): used with the infinitive of the main verb to mean (in the present tense) 'to tend to' or (in the near future) 'about to'
- *okuva* 'to come from': followed by the main verb in the infinitive, means 'just been'
- *okulema* 'to fail': used with the inifinitive to form negatives

Derivational affixes

The meaning of a verb can be altered in an almost unlimited number of ways by means of modifications to the verb stem. There are only a handful of core derivational modifications, but these can be added to the verb stem in virtually any combination, resulting in hundreds of possible compound modifications.

The passive is produced by replacing the final -*a* with -*wa* or -*ibwa*/-*ebwa*:

- *okulaba* 'to see' → *okulabwa* 'to be seen'

The reflexive is created by adding the prefix *e*- to the verb stem (equivalent to replacing the *oku*- prefix of the infinitive with *okwe*-):

- *okutta* 'to kill' → *okwetta* 'to kill oneself'

Many verbs are used only in their reflexive form:

- *okwebaka* 'to sleep' (simple form **okubaka* is not used)
- *okwetaga* 'to need' (simple form **okutaga* is not used)

Reduplication is formed by doubling the stem, and generally adds the sense of repetition or intensity:

- *okukuba* 'to strike' → *okukubaakuba* 'to batter'

The applied, or prepositional, modification, allows the verb to take an extra object and gives it the meaning 'to do for or with (someone or something). *It's formed with the infix -ir- inserted before the final -a of the stem:*

- *okukola* 'to work' → *okukolera* 'to work for (an employer)'
- *okwebaka* 'to sleep' → *okwebakira* 'to sleep on (*e.g.* a piece of furniture)'

Adding the applied infix twice gives the 'augmentative applied' modification, which has an alternative applied sense, usually further removed from the original sense than the simple applied modification:

- *okukola* 'to work' → *okukozesa* 'to utilise, employ'

The causative is formed with various changes applied to the end of the verb, usually involving the final *-a* changing to *-ya*, *-sa* or *-za*. It gives a verb the sense of 'to cause to do', and can also make an intransitive verb transitive:

- *okulaba* 'to see' → *okulabya* 'to show' (more commonly "okulaga", a different verb, is used).
- *okufuuka* 'to become' → *okufuusa* 'to turn (something or someone) into (something else)'

Appling two causative modifications results in the 'second causative':

- *okulaba* 'to see' → *okulabya* 'to show' → *okulabisa* 'to cause to show'

The neuter modification, also known as the stative, is similar to the '-able' suffix in English, except that the result is a verb meaning 'to be *x*-able' rather than an adjective meaning '*x*-able'. It's formed by inserting the infix *-ik/-ek* before the stem's final *-a*:

- *okukola* 'to do' → *okukoleka* 'to be possible'
- *okulya* 'to eat' → *okuliika* 'to be edible'

The intransitive conversive modification reverses the meaning of an intransitive verb and leaves it intransitive, or reverses the meaning of a transitive verb and makes it intransitive, similar to English's 'un-' prefix. It's formed with the infix *-uk-* inserted before the stem's final *-a*:

- *okukyala* 'to pay a visit' → *okukyaluka* 'to end one's visit, to depart'

The transitive conversive is similar to the intransitive conversive except that it results in a transitive verb. In other words it reverses the meaning of an intransitive verb and makes it transitive, or reverses the meaning of a transitive verb and leaves it transitive. It's formed with the infix *-ul-*:

- *okukola* 'to do' → *okukolula* 'to undo'
- *okusimba* 'to plant' → *okusimbula* 'to uproot'
- *okukyala* 'to pay a visit' → *okukyalula* 'to send off'

Two conversive infixes create the augmentative conversive modification:

- *okulimba* 'to deceive' → *okulimbulula* 'to disabuse, set straight'

The reciprocal modification is formed with the suffix *-na* or *-gana* (or less commonly *-ŋŋa*):

- *okulaba* 'to see' → *okulabagana* 'to see one another'
- *okutta* 'to kill' → *okuttaŋŋana* 'to kill each other'

The progressive is formed with the suffix *-nga*. It's used with finite verbs to give the sense of continuousness:

- *ndimukuuma* 'I'll look after him' → *ndimukuumanga* 'I'll always look after him'
- *tosinda* 'don't whinge' → *tosindanga* 'never whinge'
- "tobba" don't steal...."tobbanga" thou shat not steal.

This is not really a modification but a clitic, so it's always applied 'after' any grammatical inflexions.

Combinations of modifications

More than one modification can be made to a single stem:

- *okukolulika* 'to be undo-able (*i.e.* reversible)'—conversive neuter: *kola* → *kolula* → *kolulika*
- *okusimbuliza* 'to transplant'—conversive applied causative: *simba* -> *simbula* → *simbulira* → *simbuliza*
- *okulabaalabana* 'to look around oneself, be distracted'—reduplicative reciprocal: *laba* → *labaalaba* → *labaalabana*
- *okulabaalabanya* 'to distract'—reduplicative reciprocal causative: *laba* → *labaalaba* → *labaalabana* → *labaalabanya*
- *okwebakiriza* 'to pretend to sleep'—reflexive augmentative applied causative *baka* → *ebaka* → *ebakira* (applied) → *ebakirira* (augmentative applied) → *ebakiriza*

There are some restrictions that apply to the combinations in which these modifications can be made. For example the 'applied' modification can't be made to a causative stem; any causative modifications must first be removed, the applied modification made and the causative modifications then reapplied. And since the reflexive is formed with a prefix rather than a suffix, it's impossible to distinguish between, for example, reflexive causative and causative reflexive.

Numbers

The Luganda system of cardinal numbers is quite complicated. The numbers 'one' to 'five' are specialised numerical adjectives that agree with the noun they qualify. The words for 'six' to 'ten' are numerical nouns that don't agree with the qualified noun.

'Twenty' to 'fifty' are expressed as multiples of ten using the cardinal numbers for 'two' to 'five' with the plural of 'ten'. 'Sixty' to 'one hundred' are numerical nouns in their own right, derived from the same roots as the nouns for 'six' to 'ten' but with different class prefixes.

In a similar pattern, 'two hundred' to 'five hundred' are expressed as multiples of a hundred using the cardinal numbers with the plural of 'hundred'. Then 'six hundred' to 'one thousand' are nouns, again derived from the same roots as 'six' to 'ten'. The pattern repeats up to 'ten thousand', then standard nouns are used for 'ten thousand', 'one hundred thousand' and 'one million'.

The words used for this system are:

Numerical adjectives (declined to agree with the qualified noun):

- *emu* (*omu, limu, kamu, kimu, ...*) 'one'
- *bbiri* (*babiri, abiri, ...*) 'two'
- *ssatu* (*basatu, asatu, ...*) 'three'
- *nnya* (*bana, ana, ...*) 'four'
- *ttaano* (*bataano, ataano, ...*) 'five'

Numerical nouns:

- 'Six' to 'ten' (Classes II and V)
  - *mukaaga* 'six' (Class II)
  - *musanvu* 'seven'
  - *munaana* 'eight'
  - *mwenda* 'nine'
  - *kkumi* 'ten'; plural *amakumi* (Class V)
- 'Sixty' to 'one hundred' (Classes III and IV)
  - *nkaaga* 'sixty' (Class III)
  - *nsanvu* 'seventy'
  - *kinaana* 'eighty' (Class IV)
  - *kyenda* 'ninety'
  - *kikumi* 'one hundred'; plural *bikumi*
- 'Six hundred' to 'one thousand' (Class VII)
  - *lukaaga* 'six hundred'
  - *lusanvu* 'seven hundred'
  - *lunaana* 'eight hundred'
  - *lwenda* 'nine hundred'
  - *lukumi* 'one thousand'; plural *nkumi*
- 'Six thousand' to 'ten thousand' (Class VI)
  - *kakaaga* 'six thousand'
  - *kasanvu* 'seven thousand'
  - *kanaana* 'eight thousand'
  - *kenda* 'nine thousand'
  - (archaic) *kakumi* 'ten thousand'; plural *bukumi*

Standard nouns:

- *omutwalo* 'ten thousand'; plural *emitwalo* (Class II)
- *akasiriivu* 'one hundred thousand'; plural *obusiriivu* (Class VI)

- *akakadde* 'one million'; plural *obukadde* (Class VI)
- *akawumbi* 'one trillion' (1,000,000,000,000); plural *obuwumbi* (Class VI)
- *akafukunya* 'one quintillion' (1,000,000,000,000,000,000); plural *obufukunya* (Class VI)
- *akasedde* 'one septillion' (1,000,000,000,000,000,000,000,000); plural *obusedde* (Class VI)

Digits are specified from left to right, combined with *na* (following *kkumi*) and *mu* (following any other word). For example:

- 12 *kkumi na bbiri* (10 + 2)
- 22 *amakumi abiri mu bbiri* (10 × 2 + 2)
- 65 *nkaaga mu ttaano* (60 + 5)
- 122 *kikumi mu amakumi abiri mu bbiri* (100 + 10 × 2 + 2)
- 222 *bikumi bibiri mu amakumi abiri mu bbiri* (100 × 2 + 10 × 2 + 2)
- 1,222 *lukumi mu bikumi bibiri mu amakumi abiri mu bbiri* (1,000 + 100 × 2 + 10 × 2 + 2)
- 1,024 *lukumi mu amakumi abiri mu nnya* (1,000 + 10 × 2 + 4)
- 2,222 *nkumi bbiri mu bikumi bibiri mu amakumi abiri mu bbiri* (1,000 × 2 + 100 × 2 + 10 × 2 + 2)
- 2,500 *nkumi bbiri mu bikumi bitaano* (1,000 × 2 + 100 × 5)
- 7,500 *kasanvu mu bikumi bitaano* (7,000 + 100 × 5)
- 7,600 *kasanvu mu lukaaga* (7,000 + 600)
- 9,999 *kenda mu lwenda mu kyenda mu mwenda* (9,000 + 900 + 90 + 9)
- 999,000 *obusiriivu mwenda mu omutwalo mwenda mu kenda*
- 1,000,000 *akakadde* (1,000,000)
- 3,000,000 *obukadde gibiri* (1,000,000 × 3)
- 10,000,000 *obukadde kkumi* (1,000,000 × 10)
- 122,000,122 *obukadde kikumi mu amakumi abiri mu bubiri mu kikumi mu amakumi abiri mu bbiri* (1,000,000 * (100 + 10 × 2 + 2) + 100 + 10 × 2 + 2)

The numerical adjectives agree with the qualified noun:

- *emmotoka emu* 'one car' (Class III)
- *omukazi omu* 'one woman' (Class I)
- *emmotoka ataano* 'five cars'
- *abakazi bataano* 'five women'

but

- *emmotoka kikumi* 'a hundred cars'
- *abakazi kikumi* 'a hundred women'

and

- *abasajja kkumi n'omu* 'eleven men' (Class I)
- *ente kkumi n'emu* 'eleven cattle' (Class III)

The forms *emu, bbiri, ssatu, nnya* and *ttaano* are used when counting (as well as when qualifying nouns of classes III and VII).

However, a complication arises from the agreement of numerical adjectives with the powers of ten. Since the words for 'ten', 'hundred', 'thousand' and so on belong to different classes, each power of ten can be inferred from the form of the adjective qualifying it, so the plural forms of the powers of ten (*amakumi* 'tens', *bikumi* 'hundreds', *bukumi* 'tens of thousands'—but not *nkumi* 'thousands') are usually omitted, as long as this doesn't result in ambiguity.

For example:

- 40 *amakumi ana* → *ana*
- 22 *amakumi abiri mu bbiri* → *abiri mu bbiri*
- 222 *bikumi bibiri mu amakumi abiri mu bbiri* → *bibiri mu abiri mu bbiri*
- 1,024 *lukumi mu amakumi abiri mu nnya* → *lukumi mu abiri mu nnya*
- 2,222 *nkumi bbiri mu bikumi bibiri mu amakumi abiri mu bbiri* → *nkumi bbiri mu bibiri mu abiri mu bbiri*
- 2,500 *nkumi bbiri mu bikumi bitaano* → *nkumi bbiri mu bitaano*
- 7,500 *kasanvu mu bikumi bitaano* → *kasanvu mu bitaano*
- 122,000,122 *obukadde kikumi mu amakumi abiri mu bubiri mu kikumi mu amakumi abiri mu bbiri* → *obukadde kikumi mu abiri mu bubiri mu kikumi mu amakumi mu bbiri*

Note that *amanda amakumi ana* '40 batteries' cannot be shortened to *amanda ana* because this means "four batteries", and *embwa amakumi ana* '40 dogs' cannot be shortened to *embwa ana* because *ana* is the form of *nnya* used with *embwa*, so this actually means 'four dogs'! *Nkumi* 'thousands' is also not usually omitted because the form the numerical adjectives take when qualifying it is the same as the counting form, so 3,000 will always be rendered *nkumi ssatu*.

Bibliography

- Ashton, Ethel O., and others (1954) *A Luganda Grammar*, London: Longmans, Green.
- Barlon, W. Kimuli (2009) *Luganda Language: A connection with Nyanja of Zambia.* pp. 04
- Snoxall, R.A. (1967) *Luganda-English Dictionary.* Clarendon Press, Oxford
- Katamba, Francis (1993) "A new approach to tone in Luganda", in *Language.* 69. 1. pp. 33–67
- Murphy, John D. (1972) *Luganda-English Dictionary.* Catholic University of America Press
- Chesswas, J. D. (1963) *Essentials of Luganda.* Oxford University Press
- Crabtree, W. A. (1902, 1923) *Elements of Luganda Grammar.* The Uganda Bookshop/Society for Promoting Christian Knowledge
- Stevick, E.; Kamoga, F. (1970), *Luganda Pretraining Program*, Washington, DC: Foreign Service Institute

External links

- Ethnologue report for Ganda/Luganda [2]
- Luganda Basic Course [3], developed by the USA Foreign Service Institute (1968)
- *The Word in Luganda* [4], by Larry M. Hyman & Francis X. Katamba
- An excellent online summary of the Luganda language can be found at http://www.buganda.com/luganda.htm.
- Free online Luganda Dictionary on the Ganda Ancestry website http://www.gandaancestry.com/dictionary/dictionary.php
- Free online talking Luganda Dictionary and Crossword Puzzle on the Ganda portal http://www.GandaSpace.com
- Luganda - English Dictionary [5]
- The website of a team developing Luganda language capability for computers is at http://www.kizito.uklinux.net
- PanAfrican L10n page on Ganda [6]

Frank Kigozi Picareader text to speech language software.

Things to Do and See in Kampala

Kampala

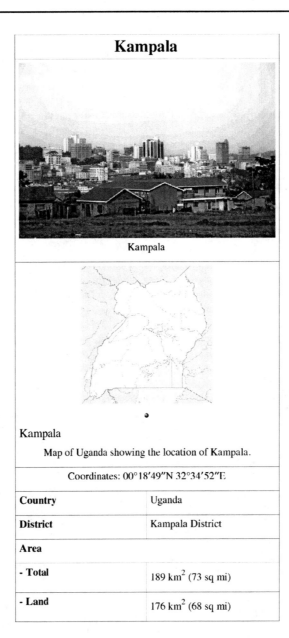

Kampala

Kampala

Kampala

Map of Uganda showing the location of Kampala.

Coordinates: 00°18′49″N 32°34′52″E	
Country	Uganda
District	Kampala District
Area	
- Total	189 km² (73 sq mi)
- Land	176 km² (68 sq mi)

- Water	13 km^2 (5 sq mi)
Elevation	1190 m (3904 ft)
Population (2008 Estimate)	
- Total	1420200
- Density	7514.3/km^2 (19461.9/sq mi)
Time zone	EAT (UTC+3)

Kampala is the largest city and capital of Uganda. The city is divided into five boroughs that oversee local planning: Kampala Central, Kawempe Division, Makindye Division, Nakawa Division and Lubaga Division. The city is coterminous with Kampala District.

History

Kampala in the early 1950s

Mutesa I, the Kabaka (king) of Buganda, had chosen the area that was to become Kampala as one of his favorite hunting grounds. The area was made up of numerous rolling hills and lush wetlands. It was an ideal breeding ground for various game, particularly a species of antelope, the impala (*Aepyceros melampus*). The origin of the word impala is likely from the Zulu language in South Africa.

The city grew as the capital of the Buganda kingdom, from which several buildings survive, including the Kasubi Tombs (built in 1881), the Buganda Parliament, the Buganda Court of Justice and the Naggalabi Buddo Coronation Site. Severely damaged in the Uganda-Tanzania War, the city has since then been rebuilt with constructions of new buildings including hotels, banks, shopping malls, educational institutions, hospitals and improvement of war torn buildings and infrastructure. Traditionally, Kampala was a city of seven hills, but over time it has come to have a lot more.

Features

The main campus of Makerere University, one of East and Central Africa's premier institutes of higher learning, can be found in the Makerere Hill area of the City. Kampala is also home to the headquarters of the East African Development Bank, located on Nakasero Hill.

Kampala is said to be built on seven hills, although this is not quite accurate.

Street in the city centre.

1. The first hill in historical importance is Kasubi Hill, which is where the Kasubi Tombs of the previous Kabakas are housed.

2. The second is Mengo Hill where the present Lubiri (Kabaka's Palace) is and the Headquarters of the Buganda Court of Justice and of the Lukiiko, Buganda's Parliament.

3. The third is Kibuli Hill, which is home to the Kibuli Mosque. Islam was brought to Uganda before the Christian missionaries came.

4. The fourth is Namirembe Hill, home to the Namirembe Anglican Cathedral. The Protestants were the first of the Christian Missions to arrive.

5. The fifth is Lubaga Hill, where the Rubaga Catholic Cathedral is, and was the headquarters of the White Fathers.

6. The sixth Nsambya, was the Headquarters of the Mill Hill Mission. It now houses Nsambya Hospital.

7. The seventh is Kampala Hill, (also known as Old Kampala), the hill of the Impala is where the ruins of Lugard's Fort were. However, the ruins were recently destroyed (2003), when the Uganda Muslim Supreme Council (UMSC) started on reconstruction of a 15,000-seater mosque on land that included the fort. The mosque was begun by Idi Amin but was never completed. The fort was then re-located to a nearby area (a new and similar one constructed), a move that has since been a source of controversy between The Historic Buildings Conservation Trust (HBCT) of Uganda and the UMSC. The UMSC was given the gazetted land as a gift by President Idi Amin in 1972 during its inauguration. This hill is where Kampala got its name.

The City spread to Nakasero Hill where the administrative centre and the wealthiest residential area is. Nakasero is also the location of the most upscale hotels in the city including:

- The Kampala Sheraton Hotel
- The Kampala Hilton Hotel
- The Kampala Serena Hotel
- The Grand Imperial Hotel
- The Imperial Royale Hotel
- The Kampala Speke Hotel

A view of suburban Kampala

There is also Tank Hill, where the water storage tanks that supply the city are located. Mulago Hill is the site of Mulago Hospital, the largest hospital in Uganda. The city is now rapidly expanding to include Makindye Hill and Konge Hill. Makindye Division incorporating Kibuli, Tank Hill and Makindye now has over 300,000 residents. Medical provision in this part of town, being more recently developed, is limited. Hospitals include Kibuli Hospital, St. Francis Hospital Nsambya and the International Hospital (IHK). Philanthropic health services are provided by Hope Clinic Lukuli situated between Tank Hill, Makindye and Konge.

Suburbs include Kololo in the east on Kololo Hill, the highest hill, home to the Uganda Museum. Other suburbs include Namirembe; Kibuli; Kabalagala; Rubaga; Ntinda; Najjera; Kisaasi; Nateete; Najjanankumbi; Kira (which incorporates Banda, Kireka, Bweyogerere, Namugongo, Bulindo and Nsasa) among others.

Other features of the city include the Uganda Museum, Ugandan National Theatre, Nakasero Market and St. Balikuddembe Market (formerly Owino Market). Kampala is also known for its nightlife, which includes several casinos, notably Casino Simba in the Garden City shopping center, Kampala Casino and Mayfair Casino. Entebbe International Airport is located at Entebbe, 35 miles (56 km) away, while Port Bell on the shores of Lake Victoria is 10 kilometres (6.2 mi) away.

Also to note is that Kampala hosts one of only seven Bahá'í Houses of Worship in the world. It is known as the Mother Temple of Africa and is situated on Kikaya Hill on the outskirts of the city. Its foundation stone was laid in January 1958, and was dedicated on January 13, 1961. See Bahá'í Faith in Uganda.

Bahá'í House of Worship in Kampala, Uganda

The Ahmadiyya Central Mosque in Kampala is the central mosque of the Ahmadiyya Muslim Community, which has 6 minarets and can hold up to 9,000 worshippers.

Kampala going westwards has Kabaka's Lubiri, the palace of the King of Buganda. Buganda is one of the oldest kingdoms in Africa, dating back to the late 13th Century. Other landmarks include the Kasubi tombs, the magnificent mosque at old Kampala, Namirembe and Rubaga Cathedral, at the very edge there is Kasumba Square Mall at the intersection of Northern Bypass and Busega roundabout.

Transportation

In early 2007, it was announced that Kampala would remove commuter taxis from its streets and replace them with a comprehensive city bus service. (It should be noted that in Kampala the term "taxi" refers to a 15-seater minibus used as public transport.) The bus service was expected to cover the greater Kampala metropolitan area including Mukono, Mpigi, Bombo, Entebbe, Wakiso and Gayaza. The decision is yet to be implemented.

Boda-bodas (local motorcycle transportation) are a popular mode of transport that gives access to many areas with in and outside the city. Standard fees for these range from UGX 500 to 1,000 or more. Boda-bodas are useful for passing through rush-hour traffic although they are usually poorly maintained and often dangerous.

In January 2007, the mayor of Kampala City announced plans to introduce a congestion fee of Sh30,000 per vehicle per day when the bus network is launched. This decision is also yet to be implemented.

Climate

Kampala features a tropical wet and dry climate, however due to city's higher altitudes, average temperatures are noticeably cooler than what is typically seen in other cities with this type of climate. Kampala seldom gets very hot during the course of the year, it's warmest month being January.

Another facet of Kampala's weather is that it features two distinct wet seasons. There is a lengthy rainy season from August through December and another shorter rainy season that begins in February and lasts through June. However, the shorter rainy season sees substantially heavier rainfall per month, with the month of April typically seeing the heaviest amount of precipitation at an average of around 175 mm of rain.

Climate data for Kampala													
Month	**Jan**	**Feb**	**Mar**	**Apr**	**May**	**Jun**	**Jul**	**Aug**	**Sep**	**Oct**	**Nov**	**Dec**	**Year**
Record high °C (°F)	33 (91)	36 (97)	33 (91)	33 (91)	29 (84)	29 (84)	29 (84)	29 (84)	31 (88)	32 (90)	32 (90)	32 (90)	36 (97)
Average high °C (°F)	28 (82)	28 (82)	27 (81)	26 (79)	25 (77)	25 (77)	25 (77)	25 (77)	27 (81)	27 (81)	27 (81)	27 (81)	26 (79)
Average low °C (°F)	18 (64)	18 (64)	18 (64)	18 (64)	17 (63)	17 (63)	17 (63)	16 (61)	17 (63)	17 (63)	17 (63)	17 (63)	17 (63)
Record low °C (°F)	12 (54)	14 (57)	13 (55)	14 (57)	15 (59)	12 (54)	12 (54)	12 (54)	13 (55)	13 (55)	14 (57)	12 (54)	12 (54)
Precipitation mm (inches)	46 (1.81)	61 (2.4)	130 (5.12)	175 (6.89)	147 (5.79)	74 (2.91)	46 (1.81)	86 (3.39)	91 (3.58)	97 (3.82)	122 (4.8)	99 (3.9)	1174 (46.22)
Source: BBC Weather													

Demographics

See also: Demographics of Uganda

Kampala has a diverse ethnic population, although the Baganda - the local ethnic group - make up over 60% of the greater Kampala region. The city's ethnic makeup has been defined by political and economic factors. During the rule of Milton Obote and Idi Amin, who were both from northern Uganda, a significant number of northern Ugandans moved into Kampala during the 1960s, 70's and 80's Most served in the armed forces and the police. Most settled around the areas where the Military and Police barracks were located - Naguru, Bugolobi and Mbuya. With the overthrow of Milton Obote in 1986, many northern Ugandans left the city. At the same time a large number of western Ugandans, particularly the Banyankole, moved into the city, reflecting the large proportion of western Ugandans in the new government of Yoweri Museveni.

The mismanagement of Uganda's economy during the 1970s and 1980s meant that there were fewer employment opportunities outside Kampala. This encouraged many people from around the country to move into the city, and most have not moved back to their home districts after the revitalization of the economy in the 1990s and 2000s.

Inter-tribal marriage in Uganda is still rare, and although many Kampala residents have been born and bred in the city they still define themselves by their tribal roots. This is more evident in the suburbs of the city, where local languages are spoken widely alongside English, Swahili and Luganda. Apart from the Baganda and Banyankole, other large ethnic groups include the Basoga, Bafumbira, Batoro, Bakiga, Alur, Bagisu, Banyoro, Iteso and Acholi.

Economy

Air Uganda has its head office in Kampala. Since assuming power in early 1986, Museveni's government has taken important steps toward economic rehabilitation. The country's infrastructure—notably its transport and communications systems which were destroyed by war and neglect—is being rebuilt. Recognizing the need for increased external support, Uganda negotiated a policy framework paper with the IMF and the World Bank in 1987. It subsequently began implementing economic policies designed to restore price stability and sustainable balance of payments, improve capacity utilization, rehabilitate infrastructure, restore producer incentives through proper price policies, and improve resource mobilization and allocation in the public sector. These policies produced positive results. Inflation, which ran at 240% in 1987 and 42% in June 1992, was 5.4% for fiscal year 1995-96 and 7.3% in 2003.

Investment as a percentage of GDP was estimated at 20.9% in 2002 compared to 13.7% in 1999. Private sector investment, largely financed by private transfers from abroad, was 14.9% of GDP in 2002. Gross national savings as a percentage of GDP was estimated at 5.5% in 2002. The Ugandan Government has also worked with donor countries to reschedule or cancel substantial portions of the country's external debts.

Uganda is a member of the WTO.

Population

The national census in 2002 estimated the population of the city at 1,189,142. The Uganda Bureau of Statistics estimated the population of Kampala at 1,420,200 in 2008.

Photos

- Photo of Kampala Road, Kampala, Uganda [1]
- Kampala at Night [2]

External links

- Kampala - City Guide and Information Portal [3]
- Ugenda Updates [4]
- Kampala City Council Website [5]
- Kampala Street Map [6]

Geographical coordinates: 00°18′49″N 32°34′52″E

pnb:کمپالا

Makindye Division

Makindye Division is one of the divisions that makes up the city of Kampala, Uganda. The city's five (5) divisions are:

- Kampala Central Division
- Kawempe Division
- Lubaga Division
- Makindye Division
- Nakawa Division

Location

Makindye Division is in the southeastern corner of the city, bordering Wakiso District to the south and west. The eastern boundary of the division is Murchison Bay, a part of Lake Victoria. Nakawa Division lies to the northeast of Makindye Division. Kampala Central Division lies to the north and Lubaga Division lies to the northeast. The coordinates of the division are:00 17N, 32 35E (Latitude:0.2791; Longitude:32.5862)

Neighborhoods in the division include Kibuye, Kabowa, Lukuli, Luwafu, Nsambya, Kansanga, Muyenga, Ggaba and Munyonyo. It is also home to the neighborhood of Kabalagala, a center for Kampala nightlife. The following landmarks are located in Makindye Division:

- Embassy of the United States
- Nsambya Hospital
- Kampala University
- Kampala International University
- Ggaba National Seminary - Roman Catholic
- Speke Resort & Conference Center
- Commonwealth Resort

See also

- Makindye
- Makindye Prison
- Kampala
- Nsambya
- Ggaba
- Kabalagala
- Lubowa
- Munyonyo

References

Geographical coordinates: 0°17′N 32°35′E

Nakasero

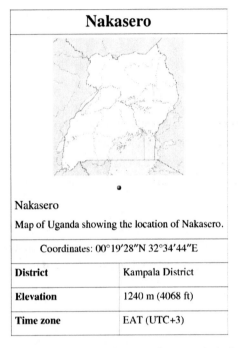

Nakasero	
Nakasero	
Map of Uganda showing the location of Nakasero.	
Coordinates: 00°19′28″N 32°34′44″E	
District	Kampala District
Elevation	1240 m (4068 ft)
Time zone	EAT (UTC+3)

Nakasero is the hill where the central business district of Kampala is located. Kampala is Uganda's capital and largest city.

Location

Nakasero is bordered by Mulago to the north, Makerere to the northwest, Old Kampala to the west, Namirembe and Mengo to the southwest, Nsambya to the south, Kibuli to the southeast and Kololo to the east. The coordinates of Nakasero Hill are: Latitude:0.3244; Longitude:32.5788.

Overview

Nakasero Hill is the location of the central business district of Kampala, Uganda's capital city (pop:1,758,543 in 2009 Est). The lower reaches of the western and southern slopes of the hill accommodate the ordinary business and commercial activities of the city. (taxi parks, train station, shopping arcades, banks and regular restaurants). Towards the top of the hill, there are government buildings including the Uganda Parliament Buildings, the Kampala City Council Building Complex and several government ministries.

The top of Nakasero Hill is the most luxurious address in the city and accommodates the most upscale hotels and restaurants in the country. The Kampala State House is also located here. The northern and eastern slopes of Nakasero Hill house the majority of Diplomatic Missions to Uganda and the residencies of most ambassadors accredited to Uganda.

Landmarks

The numerous landmarks in Kampala's central business district, located on Nakasero hill include but are not limited to the following:

Government Buildings

- Uganda Parliament Buildings
- State House, Kampala
- Headquarters of Bank of Uganda
- Headquarters of Uganda Wildlife Authority
- Uganda Bureau of Statistics
- Uganda Commercial Court Building Complex
- Uganda Government Analytical Chemistry Laboratory
- Uganda High Court
- Uganda Investment Authority
- Uganda Ministry of Finance, Planning & Economic Development
- Uganda Ministry of Foreign Affairs
- Uganda Ministry of Health
- Uganda Ministry of Internal Affairs
- Uganda Ministry of Tourism, Trade and Industry

Banking Institutions

- Headquarters of ABC Bank (Uganda)
- Headquarters of Bank of Africa (Uganda)
- Headquarters of Bank of Baroda (Uganda)
- Headquarters of Uganda Development Bank
- Headquarters of Barclays Bank (Uganda)
- Headquarters of Cairo International Bank
- Headquarters of Centenary Bank
- Headquarters of Citibank (Uganda)
- Headquarters of Crane Bank

- Headquarters of DFCU Bank
- Headquarters of Diamond Trust Bank (Uganda) Limited
- Headquarters of East African Development Bank
- Headquarters of Ecobank (Uganda)
- Headquarters of Equity Bank (Uganda)
- Headquarters of Fina Bank (Uganda)
- Headquarters of Global Trust Bank
- Headquarters of Housing Finance Bank
- Headquarters of Kenya Commercial Bank (Uganda)
- Headquarters of National Bank of Commerce (Uganda)
- Headquarters of Orient Bank - A member of the Bank PHB Group
- Headquarters of PostBank Uganda
- Headquarters of Stanbic Bank (Uganda) Limited
- Headquarters of Standard Chartered Bank (Uganda)
- Headquarters of Tropical Bank
- Headquarters of Uganda Development Bank
- Headquarters of United Bank for Africa

Hotels, Clubs & Casinos

- Casino Paradise
- Grand Imperial Hotel
- Emin Pasha Hotel
- Fairway Hotel
- Hotel Equatoria
- Imperial Royale Hotel
- Kampala Casino
- Kampala Club
- Kampala Hilton Hotel
- Movenpick Hotel Kampala
- Kampala Serena Hotel
- Kampala Sheraton Hotel
- Mamba Point Hotel
- Park Hotel
- Uganda Doctors Club
- Kampala Speke Hotel

Foreign Embassies

- Embassy of Austria
- Embassy of Belgium
- Embassy of Cuba
- Embassy of Denmark
- Embassy of France
- Embassy of Finland
- Embassy of India
- Embassy of Ireland
- Embassy of Italy
- Embassy of Kenya
- Embassy of Nigeria
- Embassy of Norway
- Embassy of Somalia
- Embassy of South Korea
- Embassy of Spain
- Embassy of Switzerland
- Embassy of Tanzania

Places of Worship

- All Saints Cathedral - Anglican
- Christ the King Church - Roman Catholic

Others

- Buganda Road Primary School
- Headquarters of AMREF in Uganda
- Headquarters of UNDP in Uganda
- Kampala Central Police Station
- Kampala City Council Building Complex
- Kampala Railway Station
- Nakasero Farmers Market
- Uganda Main Post Office
- Uganda National Cultural Center
- Uganda Securities Exchange
- Nakasero Hospital Ltd

External links

- About Nakasero Market [1]

Photos

- Nakasero Farmers Market [2]

See also

- Kampala
- Kololo
- Muyenga
- Mulago
- Mengo
- Makerere
- Nsambya
- Government of Uganda

References

Geographical coordinates: 0°19′28″N 32°34′44″E

Kawempe Division

Kawempe Division is one of the divisions that makes up the city of Kampala, Uganda. The city's five (5) divisions are:

- Kampala Central Division
- Kawempe Division
- Lubaga Division
- Makindye Division
- Nakawa Division

Location

Kawempe Division is in the northwestern corner of the city, bordering Wakiso District] to the west, north and east, Nakawa Division to the southeast, and Kampala Central to the south, and Lubaga Division to the southwest. The coordinates of the division are:00 23N, 32 33E (Latitude:0.3792; Longitude:32.5574). Neighborhoods in the division include Kawempe, Jinja-Kawempe, Kanyanya, Kazo, Mpereerwe, Kisaasi, Kikaya and Kyebando.

Landmarks

The following landmarks are located in Kawempe Division:

- Bahai Temple
- Bugisu Industries - A manufacturer of packaging materials

External links

- Challenges and Constraints to Planning and Development in Kampala [1]

See also

- Kawempe
- Kampala
- Makerere
- Nakasero
- Mulago

References

Geographical coordinates: 00°23′N 32°33′E

Kasubi hill

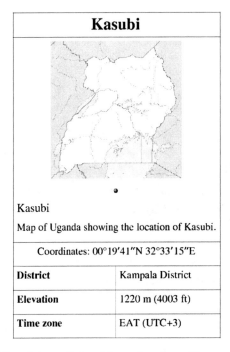

Kasubi	
Kasubi	
Map of Uganda showing the location of Kasubi.	
Coordinates: 00°19′41″N 32°33′15″E	
District	Kampala District
Elevation	1220 m (4003 ft)
Time zone	EAT (UTC+3)

Kasubi is a hill in Kampala, Uganda's capital and largest metropolitan area.

Location

Kasubi is bordered by Kawaala to the north, Makerere to the east, Naakulabye to the southeast, Lusaze to the southwest, Lubya to the west and Namungoona to the northwest. This location is approximately 5.5 kilometres (3.4 mi), by road, northwest of Kampala's central business district. The coordinates of Kasubi are:00 19 41N, 32 33 15E (Latitude:0.3280; Longitude:32.5540).

History

Prior to 1856, Kasubi Hill was known as Nabulagala. Sometime after that date, Kabaka Muteesa I Mukaabya, having met misfortune at Banda Hill, where he had built his first palace, relocated to Nabulagala. He re-named the hill **Kasubi**, after the ancestral village of his mother, located in then **Kyaggwe County**; what today is known as Mukono District. Today, Buganda traditionalists refer to the place interchangeably as **Kasubi** or **Nabulagala** or **Kasubi-Nabulagala**.

After his death in 1884, Kabaka Muteesa I was buried at Kasubi, the first Kabaka to be buried there. Since then, Kasubi has become the official royal burial site of the Buganda monarchy. The Kasubi Royal Tombs are recognised as a World Heritage Site and is of very high significance in the culture of the Baganda.

Overview

Kasubi Hill is a royal cultural site of the Kingdom of Buganda, one of he constitutional traditional monarchies in 21st century Uganda.

Landmarks

Main article: Kasubi Tombs

Today, the most important landmark on Kasubi Hill are the Kasubi Royal Tombs, the official burial place of the Kings of Buganda. As of January 2010, four (4) consecutive Kings of Buganda are buried at Kasubi

- Kabaka Muteesa I Mukaabya in 1884
- Kabaka Mwanga II Mukasa, died in exile in 1903, re-buried at Kasubi in 1910.
- Kabaka Sir Daudi Chwa II in 1939 and
- Kabaka Sir Edward Muteesa II, died in exile in 1969, re-buried at Kasubi in 1971.
- Other landmarks include Kasubi Medical Clinic, a community health clinic operated by *Hope Medical Clinics Uganda Limited*, a Ugandan charitable organisation, founded by two Americans.
- A branch of Pride Microfinance Limited

External links

- About Kasubi Medical Clinic [1]

See also

- Kasubi Tombs
- Kabaka of Buganda
- Muteesa I of Buganda
- Mwanga II of Buganda
- Daudi Chwa II of Buganda
- Muteesa II of Buganda

References

Geographical coordinates: 00°19′41″N 32°33′15″E

Nakawa Division

Nakawa Division is one of the divisions that makes up the city of Kampala, Uganda. The division takes its name from Nakawa, where the division headquarters are located.

Location

Nakawa Division is in the eastern part of the city, bordering Kira Town to the east, Wakiso District to the north, Kawempe Division to the northwest, Kampala Central to the west, Makindye Division across Murchison Bay to the southwest and Lake Victoria to the south. The coordinates of the division are:00 20N, 32 37E (Latitude:0.3337; Longitude:32.6180). Neighborhoods in the division include Nakawa, Mbuya, Bugoloobi, Luzira, Butabika, Mutungo, Ntinda, Kigoowa, Kyambogo, Kiwaatule, Bbuye and Kulambiro. Nakawa Division covers an area of 47.45 square kilometres (18.32 sq mi).

Overview

The topography of the division is characterized by flat-topped hills of uniform height divided by shallow valleys forming papyrus swamps. Most of the streams flow into Lake Victoria. The streams are characterized by low gradient and comparatively broad valley floors. Owing to alluvial aggregation, low gradient and frequent local tilting, many valley floors have become seasonal or permanent swamps. The soil geology from which the soils of the corridor formed belongs to the Basement Complex. It consists of a variety of metamorphic largely granitoid rocks, acid gneisses, schists and sand stones. Most of these rocks are highly weathered.

The meteorological data for Kampala City is typical of Nakawa Division. The division is characterized by comparatively small seasonal variations in temperature. Due to a high rate of evaporation from the lake surface and to regular winds, which drift across the lake from east to west all seasons, the average rainfall is high 1558 millimetres (61.3 in). There is a tendency of the rainfall to decrease as one moves northwards from the lake shores. The rain falls in 160 to 170 days each year, with two peaks from March to May and from October to November.

Only a small proportion of the division vegetation can be considered as natural. The vegetation of the hills which was originally shrubs and forests has been modified to a greater extent as a result of clearing to give way for settlement (high income residential neighborhoods on the hills) and the papyrus swamps have been encroached on, in the valleys, by illegal developers.

Demographics

The 1991 national census estimated the population in the division at 135,519 people. The 2002 census put the figure at 246,781 people, with 122,249 (49.5%) females and 124,532 (50.5%) males. In 2002, Nakawa Division contributed 20.3% of the total Kampala District population. Children below five (5) years of age contributed 20% of the total Division population. The youth aged 10 to 24 contributed to 30% of the total population and 26.7% of the population were women of child-bearing age. The population growth rate in 2002 was 4.8% and the total fertility rate was 5.1 %. The average family size is 4 and the maternal mortality rate is equivalent to 265 per 100,000 live births.

Population trends

Using the data above, it is estimated that the population in Nakawa Division in 2010 is approximately 359,100. See table below:

Nakawa Division Population Trends

Year	Estimated Population
2002	246,800
2003	258,600
2004	271,000
2005	284,000
2006	297,700
2007	312,000
2008	326,900
2009	342,600
2010	359,100
2011	376,300
2012	394,400

Landmarks

The following landmarks are located in Nakawa Division:
- Kyambogo University
- Makerere University Business School
- Commercial Plaza Shopping Complex
- Headquarters of Uganda Revenue Authority
- Headquarters of Uganda Ministry of Defense
- Mbuya Hospital - One of the two Military Hospitals in Uganda
- Butabika National Referral Hospital - Uganda's only psychiatric referral hospital
- Port Bell - With its breweries and lakeside port
- Luzira Maximum Security Prison - Over 10,000 inmates including 300 on death row

External links

- Challenges and Constraints to Planning and Development in Kampala [1]

See also

- Kampala
- Kawempe Division
- Makindye Division
- Kololo

References

Geographical coordinates: 00°20′N 32°37′E

Lubaga Division

Lubaga Division is one of the divisions that makes up the city of Kampala, Uganda. The division takes its name from Lubaga, where the division headquarters are located. The city's five (5) divisions are:

- Kampala Central Division
- Kawempe Division
- Lubaga Division
- Makindye Division
- Nakawa Division

Location

Lubaga Division is in the western part of the city, bordering Wakiso District to the west and south of the division. The eastern boundary of the division is Kampala Central Division. Kawempe Division lies to the north of Lubaga Division. The coordinates of the division are:00 18N, 32 33E (Latitude:0.3029; Longitude:32.5529). Neighborhoods in the division include Mutundwe, Nateete, Lungujja, Busega, Lubaga, Mengo, Namungoona, Lubya, Lugala, Bukesa, Naakulabye, Kasubi and Kawaala.

Landmarks

The following landmarks are located in Lubaga Division:

- St. Mary's Catholic Cathedral
- Residence of the Cardinal of Kampala
- Residence of the Archbishop of Kampala Archdiocese
- Lubaga Hospital - A 300-bed community hospital administered by the Catholic Archdiocese of Kampala
- Lubaga Nurses School
- Lubaga Miracle Center - A Pentecostal Congregation Church
- Pope Paul VI Memorial Community Center
- Headquarters of Lubaga Division
- Mengo Palace - The Lubiri is located in Lubaga Division
- Bulange Office Complex - Houses the Buganda Parliament and offices of the Kabaka of Buganda

See also

- Lubaga
- Mengo
- Kampala
- Nakasero

References

Geographical coordinates: 00°18′N 32°33′E

Kasubi Tombs

<table>
<tr><td colspan="2" align="center">Kasubi Tombs*</td></tr>
<tr><td colspan="2" align="center">UNESCO World Heritage Site</td></tr>
<tr><td colspan="2" align="center"></td></tr>
<tr><td>State Party</td><td>▬ Uganda</td></tr>
<tr><td>Type</td><td>Cultural</td></tr>
<tr><td>Criteria</td><td>i, iii, iv, vi</td></tr>
<tr><td>Reference</td><td>1022 [1]</td></tr>
<tr><td>Region**</td><td>Africa</td></tr>
<tr><td>Coordinates</td><td>0°19′45″N 32°33′12″E</td></tr>
<tr><td colspan="2" align="center">Inscription history</td></tr>
<tr><td>Inscription</td><td>2001 (25th Session)</td></tr>
<tr><td colspan="2">* Name as inscribed on World Heritage List. [2]
** Region as classified by UNESCO. [3]</td></tr>
</table>

The **Kasubi Tombs** in Kampala, Uganda, is the site of the burial grounds for four kabakas (kings of Buganda), and a UNESCO World Heritage Site.

On 16 March 2010, some of the major buildings there were almost completely destroyed by a fire, the cause of which is under investigation. The outraged Buganda Kingdom has vowed to rebuild the tombs of their kings and President Museveni said the national government of Uganda would assist in the restoration of the site.

Tombs

The royal enclosure at Kasubi Hill, also known as the Ssekabaka's Tombs, was first built in 1881. The circular site contained many structures, including the royal tombs of four Kabakas of Buganda. The tombs were held in straw thatched buildings. The site remains an important spiritual and political site for the Baganda people. In 2001, the Kasubi Tombs were declared a UNESCO World Heritage Site .

The kabakas buried at the site were:

- Muteesa I (1835–1884)
- Mwanga II (1867–1903)
- Daudi Chwa II (1896–1939)
- Sir Edward Muteesa II (1924–1969).

Destruction

On 16 March 2010, at about 8.30 pm local time, the Kasubi tombs were destroyed by fire. The cause of the fire is as yet unknown. The Buganda kingdom has promised to conduct independent investigations into the fire, alongside the national police force.

John Bosco Walusimbi, Prime Minister of the Buganda kingdom, stated on 17 March:

> The kingdom is in mourning. There are no words to describe the loss occasioned by this most callous act.
>
> —*The Guardian*

The interior of the Muzibu Azaala Mpanga included relics and portraits of the buried kabakas

The remains of the kabakas are intact, according to Walusimbi, as the inner sanctum of the tombs was protected from total destruction.

On 17 March 2010, His Majesty the Kabaka of Buganda, Ronald Muwenda Mutebi II, and the President of Uganda, Yoweri Museveni, visited the site of the tombs. Hundreds of people have also travelled to the site to help salvage any remains.

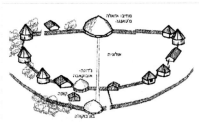

The structure containing the tombs was located at the end of a large courtyard

During the President's visit, riots broke out. Security forces shot dead two rioters and five were reportedly injured. The Ugandan soldiers and police also clashed with rioters in the capital city of Kampala. Forces used tear gas to disperse rioters of the Baganda ethnic group.

The destruction occurred in the midst of an awkward relationship between the government of Uganda and the Buganda kingdom, particularly in light of the September 2009 riots. Ahead of these riots, the king of Buganda Ronald Mutebi Mwenda was stopped from touring parts of his kingdom, and several journalists who were allegedly sympathetic to the kingdom and the rioters were arrested and are awaiting trial.

The administration of the Buganda Kingdom has vowed to rebuild the tombs and President Museveni said the national government would assist in the restoration.

External links

- ♨ Media related to Kasubi Tombs at Wikimedia Commons
- Tombs of Buganda Kings at Kasubi [5], UNESCO World Heritage Centre
- Kasubi Tombs [6]
- Kasubi Tombs Digital Media Archive [7] (creative commons-licensed photos, laser scans, panoramas), using data from a Skybucket 3D/Plowman-Craven/CyArk research partnership
- Fire Destroys Kasubi Tombs [8], Uganda *Daily Monitor*, 17 March 2010

Data from a laser scanning project held in early 2009 produced detailed architectural models of Muzibu Azaala Mpanga, the main building at the complex and tomb of the Kabakas. This data will help in the building's reconstruction. See "Royal Kasubi Tombs Destroyed in Fire" [4]. CyArk Blog. Retrieved 19 March 2010.

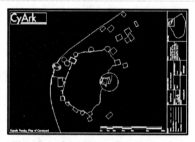

Plan view of the Oluyga Courtyard, using data from the laser scanning project in early 2009

Mengo, Uganda

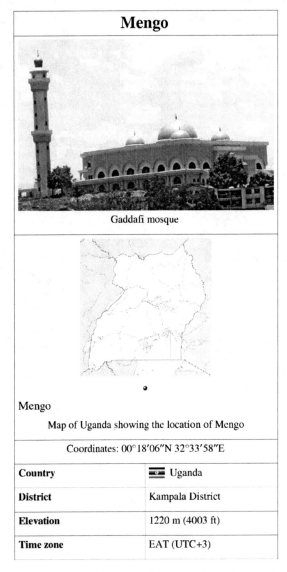

Mengo

Gaddafi mosque

Mengo

Map of Uganda showing the location of Mengo

Coordinates: 00°18′06″N 32°33′58″E

Country	🇺🇬 Uganda
District	Kampala District
Elevation	1220 m (4003 ft)
Time zone	EAT (UTC+3)

Mengo is a hill in Lubaga Division, Kampala, Uganda's capital and largest city.

Location

Mengo is bordered by Kampala Hill to the north, Nsambya Hill to the east, Kibuye to the southeast, Ndeeba to the south, Lubaga Hill to the west and Namirembe Hill to the northwest. The coordinates of Mengo Hill are:00 18 06N, 32 33 58E (Latitude:0.3015; Longitude:32.5660). The peak of the hill is at 1210 metres (3970 ft) above sea level.

Overview

Mengo Hill is the location of the main palace (known as Lubiri or Mengo Palace) of the Kabaka (King) of the Kingdom of Buganda, an ancient traditional African monarchy that dates back almost 800 years. Mengo has been the main palace since it was first constructed in 1885 by Danieri Mwanga II Mukasa, the 31st Kabaka of Buganda. Measuring 4 square miles (10 km^2) in size, the palace is ringed by a six-foot brick fence and has a small airstrip within its walls.

Mengo Hill has played an important role in Ugandan political and religious history. "Mengo" is a Luganda word for grinding stones. Legend has it that ancient migrant communities from Ssese Islands who settled on the hill used these stones to grind their food. It is here that the Buganda Agreement of 1900 was signed between the Kabaka of Buganda and British colonial officials establishing the Uganda Protectorate.

The history of Mengo Hill is also entwined with that of adjacent Namirembe Hill, the seat of the Anglican Church of Uganda, because of the monarchy's close association with the Church of England. The *Bulange*, which houses offices for the Kabaka and the *Lukiiko* (Buganda Parliament), is located at the base of Namirembe Hill. The building was constructed between 1953 and 1958 by Sir Edward Muteesa II, at a cost of US$5 million; a colossal sum at that time. Also located on Namirembe Hill is Mengo Hospital, a private, non-profit community hospital administered by the Anglican Church in Uganda.

Landmarks

Landmarks on Mengo Hill or near the hill include:

- The main palace of the King of Buganda, the *Lubiri*.
- *Bulange*, the The Parliament Building of the Buganda Parliament (the *Lukiiko*). Moved outside of the palace to the adjacent Namirembe Hill, to accommodate the size of a modern building in 1958. The building also houses the offices of the Kabaka of Buganda
- The Kabaka's Lake, a man-made lake approximately 5 acres (2.0 ha), for the personal use and enjoyment of the Kabaka; located just outside the main palace entrance.
- Mengo Hospital - A 300-bed private hospital, affiliated with the Church of Uganda; located at adjacent Namirembe Hill

- The Joint Clinical Research Center - Located adjacent to the palace, the medical research center is housed in the *Butikkiro*, the former official residence of the Prime Minister of Buganda (*Katikkiro*). This building is one of Buganda's assets that have yet to be returned to the Kingdom.
- The main campus of St. Lawrence University (Uganda) - Located close to the Kabaka's Lake.
- The Buildings of the Uganda Court of Appeal
- Namirembe Hill - Adjacent to and immediately northwest of Mengo Hill. It is the location of St. Paul's Cathedral, the most prominent Anglican place of worship in Buganda

External links

- The Brandt Travel Guide - Descriptions of Mengo and Environs [1]
- Official Website of the Kingdom of Buganda [2]

Photos

- Photo of the Buganda Parliament Building (Bulange) [3]
- Photo of the "Twekobe", the Kabaka's residence within Mengo Palace [4]

See also

- Kampala
- Kabaka of Buganda
- Lubaga
- Lubaga Division
- Battle of Mengo Hill

References

Geographical coordinates: 00°20′48″N 32°36′20″E

Kibuli

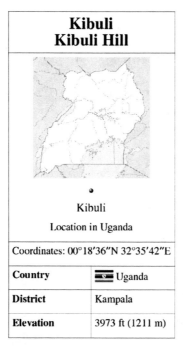

Kibuli Kibuli Hill	
Kibuli Location in Uganda	
Coordinates: 00°18′36″N 32°35′42″E	
Country	Uganda
District	Kampala
Elevation	3973 ft (1211 m)

Kibuli is a hill in the center of Kampala, the capital and largest city in Uganda.

Location

Kibuli Hill is bordered by Kololo to the north, Nakawa and Mbuya to the northeast, Namuwongo to the east, Muyenga to the southeast, Kabalagala to the south, Nsambya to the southwest, the Queen's Clock Tower to the east and Nakasero to the northeast. Kibuli is located approximately 3.5 miles (5.6 km) southeast of Kampala's central business district. The coordinates of Kibuli Hill are: 00 18 36N, 32 35 42 (Latitude:0.3100; Longitude:32.5950).

Overview

Kibuli Hill rises to a peak of 3973 feet (1211 m), above sea level. Prince Badru Kakungulu, a member of the Buganda Royal Family owned most of the hill, before he donated it to the Ugandan Moselem community. That land today houses the Kibuli Mosque, Kibuli Secondary School, Kibuli Hospital and Kibuli Teacher Training College. The hill also accommodates a police training school and a teacher training college. At the base of the hill, on the eastern side of Kibuli, is the neighborhood called Namuwongo, the location of the old Industrial Area of the city and the oil depots of three major oil companies; Shell, Total, and Caltex.

Landmarks

The landmarks on Kibuli Hill include:

- Kibuli Hospital
- Kibuli Mosque
- Kibuli Secondary School - A mixed day and boarding secondary school
- Kibuli Teacher Training College
- Greenhill Academy - An upscale private school (Grades: PreK through Grade 13)
- Uganda Police Training Academy
- A campus of the Islamic University in Uganda (IUIU)
- Kibuli Central Market

External links

- Kibuli Hill Portal [1]

See also

- Kibuli Hospital
- Kampala
- Kololo
- Nakasero
- Nsambya
- Kabalagala

References

Geographical coordinates: 00°18′36″N 32°35′42″E

Namirembe hill

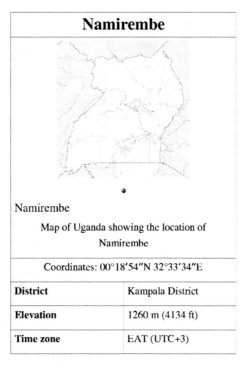

Namirembe	
Namirembe	
Map of Uganda showing the location of Namirembe	
Coordinates: 00°18′54″N 32°33′34″E	
District	Kampala District
Elevation	1260 m (4134 ft)
Time zone	EAT (UTC+3)

Namirembe is a hill in Kampala, Uganda's capital and largest city. It is also a common name given to girls in several Baganda clans. Namirembe comes from the Luganda word "mirembe" meaning "peace". Namirembe loosely translates into *Full of Peace*. Legend has it that this hill was a gathering place for celebrating peace or war victory.

Location

Namirembe is bordered by Makerere to the northeast, Old Kampala to the east, Mengo to the southeast, Lubaga to the southwest, Lungujja to the west, Kasubi to the northwest and Naakulabye to the north. The coordinates of Namirembe Hill are:00 18 54N, 32 33 34E (Latitude:0.3150; Longitude:32.5595). The distance, by road, from the central business district of Kampala to Namirembe is approximately 2 kilometres (1.2 mi).

History

Namirembe Hill has been the location of the main Anglican place of worship in Buganda since Bishop Alfred Tucker established the offices of the Diocese of Eastern Equatorial Africa in 1890. Tragedy befell the first four (4) church structures:

1. The first church building, constructed in 1890, with a capacity of 800 people was abandoned in 1891 because it was located in a swampy area at the base of Namirembe Hill. Also, a bigger building was needed to accommodate the ever growing congregation.
2. The second church building was constructed from July 1891 until July 1892, with a seating capacity of 3,000+. In October 1894, strong winds during a thunderstorm blew the roof off of the church and it was ruined.
3. The third church building was built between 1894 and 1895. It had a seating capacity of about 4,000 worshipers. That building, constructed with traditional African materials, was abandoned in the early 1900s due to fear that termites would destroy the building.
4. The fourth church building was constructed with earthen brick walls and a thatched roof, between 1900 and 1904. At the opening ceremony, on Tuesday 21 June 1904, an estimated 10,000 people were in attendance. The congregation included Kabaka Daudi Chwa II, aged 7 years old at that time. On the afternoon of Friday 23 September 1910, the roof was gutted by a fire which started when lightning struck the building. Within less than 30 minutes, the entire roof was destroyed and the church was ruined.
5. The current cathedral (St. Paul's Cathedral) was constructed between 1915 and 1919 using earthen bricks and earthen roof tiles. The cathedral is still standing, needing repairs from time to time, as expected.

Overview

The hill rises 4134 feet (1260 m) above sea level. It stands adjacent to Mengo Hill, the seat of the Buganda Government. The history of the two hills is intertwined, geographically, politically and religiously.

Namirembe is the location of St. Paul's Cathedral, the main place of worship of the Anglican Church in Uganda, from the time of its construction (1915 to 1919), until the 1960's when the Cathedral became the seat of the Diocese of Namirembe. At that time, the headquarters of the Church of Uganda moved to All Saints Church in Nakasero. The Anglican Faith is the religion most closely associated with the Buganda Monarchy since the end of the religious wars of the 1890s.

Mengo Hospital (also known as Namirembe Hospital), the first hospital in Uganda, was started by Sir Albert Ruskin Cook in May 1897. At the northwestern base of Namirembe Hill are the Buganda royal burial grounds known as Kasubi Tombs. It is here, that the kings of Buganda are buried.

The *Bulange*, Buganda's parliament building is also situated on Namirembe Hill, just across from Mengo hill. The Mengo Palace on Mengo Hill is connected to the Bulange on Namirembe Hill by a straight road, about a mile long, called **Kabaka Anjagala Road** (The King Loves Me). About halfway, the straight road is intersected by *Lubaga Road*. There is a roundabout for the use of ordinary travelers. However, there is a strait-way through the roundabout with a gate. That is for the exclusive use of the Kabaka when moving between the palace and the parliament building. Tradition forbids the king from going round the roundabout. He must travel straight when moving between the two locations.

Landmarks

Landmarks on Namirembe Hill or near the hill include:

* St. Paul's Cathedral - The most prominent place of worship in the Anglican Church in Uganda
* Residence of the Archbishop of the Church of Uganda
* Residence of the Bishop of Namirembe Anglican Diocese
* Sanyu Babies Home - An Orphanage managed by a private NGO
* Mengo Hospital - A 300 community hospital affiliated with the Church of Uganda
* The Bulange Complex - The parliamentary building that houses the parliament of Buganda, known as the *Lukiiko* and the offices of the Kabaka of Buganda.

External links

* About Namirembe Hill [1]

Photos

* Photo of Namirembe Cathedral [2]

See also

* Kampala
* Mengo
* Lubaga
* Kasubi

References

Geographical coordinates: 00°18′54″N 32°33′34″E

Lubaga

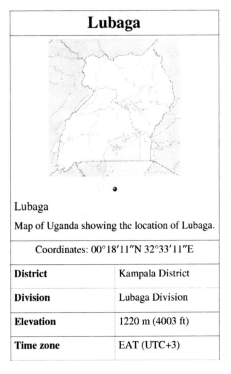

Lubaga	
Map of Uganda showing the location of Lubaga.	
Coordinates: 00°18′11″N 32°33′11″E	
District	Kampala District
Division	Lubaga Division
Elevation	1220 m (4003 ft)
Time zone	EAT (UTC+3)

Lubaga is a hill in Kampala, Uganda's capital and largest city. Its comes from the Luganda word *okubaga*, a process of "planning" or "making a structure stronger" while constructing it. For example; *okubaga ekisenge* means to strengthen the internal structure of a wall while building a house.

Location

Lubaga is bordered by Mengo to the east, Namirembe to the northeast, Kasubi to the north, Lubya to the northwest, Lungujja and Busega to the west, Nateete to the southwest Mutundwe to the south and Ndeeba to the southeast. The coordinates of Lubaga are:00 18 11N, 32 33 11E (Latitude:03029; Longitude:32.5529). The distance, by road, from the central business district of Kampala to Lubaga is approximately 3 kilometres (1.9 mi).

History

The hill served as location of one of the palaces of the King of Buganda from the 18th century. Kabaka Ndawula Nsobya, the nineteenth (19th) Kabaka of Buganda, who ruled from 1724 until 1734, maintained his capital on Lubaga Hill.

The palace on Lubaga Hill was used to plan military expeditions by Buganda's generals. However, the late 19th century, during the reign of Muteesa I Mukaabya Walugembe Kayiira, the palace caught fire and was abandoned. When the Catholic White Fathers came calling in 1879, they were allocated land nearby. Eventually they were given land on Lubaga Hill itself where they built a cathedral, beginning in 1914 which was completed in 1925.

However, the early missionaries had problems pronouncing the word *Lubaga*, as it is correctly spelled. They instead pronounced it with an "r" as in **Rubaga**. In Luganda, there is no word that starts with an "R" or "X" or "Q". Other Bantu languages from western Uganda and the African Great Lakes Area however, do have words starting with "R".

Overview

Lubaga hill was the location of the main palace of Kabaka Muteesa I who ruled Buganda between 1856 and 1884. The palace was struck by lightning and was rebuilt on neighboring Mengo Hill. The first Roman Catholic missionaries to arrive in Buganda were Frenchmen, Father Pierre Lourdel Monpel and Brother Amans, who settled near the hill in 1879

As the Catholic Church took root in the country, the missionaries were allocated land on Lubaga Hill. The construction of **St. Mary's Cathedral** on Lubaga Hill took place between 1914 and 1925, with the assistance of monetary contributions from Roman Catholic congregations abroad. Later, the missionaries also built a hospital and a nursing school on the hill.

Today, Lubaga remains the seat of the headquarters of the Catholic Church in Uganda. It is the seat of the Roman Catholic Archdiocese of Kampala. The remains of the first African Catholic bishop in Uganda, Bishop Joseph Nakabaale Kiwanuka and those of the first African Catholic Cardinal, Cardinal Emmanuel Kiwanuka Nsubuga are kept in the Catholic Mission on the hill.

Landmarks

Landmarks on Lubaga Hill or near the hill include:

- St. Mary's Catholic Cathedral
- Residence of the Cardinal of Kampala
- Residence of the Archbishop of Kampala Archdiocese
- Lubaga Hospital - A 300-bed community hospital administered by the Catholic Archdiocese of Kampala
- Lubaga Nurses School
- Lubaga Miracle Center - A Pentecostal Congregation Church
- Pope Paul VI Memorial Community Center
- Headquarters of Lubaga Division - One of the five (5) administrative divisions of the city of Kampala.

External links

- About Lubaga Hill [1]

Photos

- Artist's Impression of The Capital of Buganda on Rubaga Hill in the mid 1800's [2]
- Photo of St. Mary's Cathedral, Lubaga [3]

See also

- Lubaga Division
- Kampala

References

Geographical coordinates: 00°18′11″N 32°33′11″E

Kampala Hill

Kampala Hill	
Nickname(s): Old Kampala	
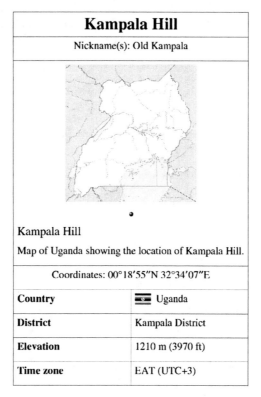	
Kampala Hill	
Map of Uganda showing the location of Kampala Hill.	
Coordinates: 00°18′55″N 32°34′07″E	
Country	▦ Uganda
District	Kampala District
Elevation	1210 m (3970 ft)
Time zone	EAT (UTC+3)

Kampala Hill, commonly referred to as **Old Kampala**, is a hill in the center of Kampala, Uganda's capital and largest city.

Location

Kampala Hill is bordered by Makerere to the north, Nakasero to the east, Mengo to the south and Namirembe to the west. The coordinates of the hill are 00°18′55″N, 32°34′07″E (Latitude: 0.3153; Longitude: 32.5685). When calculating distances between Kampala and other places, **Kampala Hill** is often taken as the starting point.

History

Before the arrival of the British, Kampala Hill, along with the neighboring environs, was a favorite hunting ground of the King of Buganda. The area was particularly rich with game, especially Impala, a type of African antelope. The word **Impala,** most probably comes from the Zulu language. The British referred to the hill as the **Hill of the Impala**. The Luganda translation comes to *Akasozi K'empala*.

Through repeated usage, the name of the place eventually became **Kampala**. The name then came to apply to the entire city.

Frederick Lugard, the British soldier who arrived in Uganda in the 1890s, built his fort on top of the hill. The original fort was relocated to a different site on the hill in 2003, to accommodate the largest mosque in Uganda, with a seating capacity of 15,000 people, built with monetary assistance from Libya. The completed mosque was opened officially in June 2007.

Overview

Kampala hill was the nucleus of the city of Kampala. When the city expanded to other neighboring hills, the place began to be referred to as Old Kampala, a name that is still in use today, 120 years later. As of 2010, the hill is a mixed commercial and residential neighborhood with high-rise apartment complexes, shops, restaurants, bars, cafes, bed-and-breakfast establishments and several motels. The neighborhood is a beehive of activity, both during the week and on weekeds.

Landmarks

Landmarks on Kampala Hill or near the hill include:

- The site where St. Matiya Mulumba was murdered on 30 May 1886 - One of the Uganda Martyrs
- The Uganda Moslem Supreme Council Mosque - The largest mosque in Uganda; seating capacity 15,000.
- Fort Lugard - Built in the 1890s, by Lord Lugard, the first military administrator of the British East Africa Company
- Old Kampala Hospital - A private hospital
- Old Kampala Senior Secondary School - A non-residential public high school
- A branch of Diamond Trust Bank (Uganda) Limited
- Nana Hostel - An upscale residential hostel for affluent university students
- Old Kampala Police Station
- The Headquarters of the Uganda Muslim Supreme Council
- Nakivubo Stadium - Seating capacity 25,000, located in the valley between Kampala Hill, Nakasero and Mengo

External links

- About Kampala Hill [1]

See also

- Kampala
- Nakasero
- Mengo
- Namirembe
- Kampala District

References

Geographical coordinates: 00°18′55″N 32°34′07″E

Kampala Sheraton Hotel

Kampala Sheraton Hotel	
Location	Kampala, Uganda
Opening date	1965
Rooms	218

Kampala Sheraton Hotel is a hotel in Kampala, Uganda. It is located in the heart of Kampala and has 218 rooms. It was built in 1965 as the Apollo Hotel.

Makindye

Makindye	
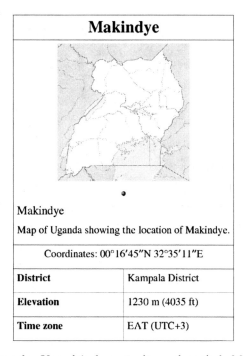 Makindye Map of Uganda showing the location of Makindye.	
Coordinates: 00°16′45″N 32°35′11″E	
District	Kampala District
Elevation	1230 m (4035 ft)
Time zone	EAT (UTC+3)

Makindye is a hill in Kampala, Uganda's largest city and capital. Makindye is also the seat of Makindye Division, one of the five administrative zones of the city of Kampala. The other four divisions are:

- Kampala Central Division
- Nakawa Division
- Kawempe Division
- Lubaga Division

Location

Makindye is bordered by Nsambya to the north, Kibuye to the northwest, Najjanankumbi to the west, Lubowa in Wakiso District to the south, Luwafu to the southeast and Lukuli to the east. Kansanga and Kabalagala lie to Makindye's northeast. The coordinates of Makindye are:00 16 45N, 32 11E (Latitude:0.2791; Longitude:32.5862). The road distance between Makindye and the central business district of Kampala is about 7 kilometres (4.3 mi).

Overview

Makindye at its peak, stands 1230 metres (4040 ft) above sea level. It affords a commanding view of the surrounding areas of the city and of neighboring parts of Wakiso District. It also affords a view of Murchison Bay, a part of Lake Victoria to the east and southeast of Makindye. The residential areas on Makindye hill are of middle class proportions. Many of the homes have adjacent plots of land which are often used to grow vegetables.

Landmarks

Landmarks on Makindye Hill or near the hill include:

- Headquarters of Makindye Division
- Makindye Military Police Barracks
- Makindye Foursquare Gospel Church - A place of worship affiliated with the Pentecostal Movement
- Makindye General Hospital - A public hospital administered by the Uganda Ministry of Health (Construction begins 2011)

Photos

- Photo of Gas Station in Makindye [1]

See also

- Kampala
- Makindye Division
- Nsambya
- Kabalagala
- Lubowa
- Makindye Prison

References

Geographical coordinates: 00°16′45″N 32°35′11″E

Kololo

Kololo	
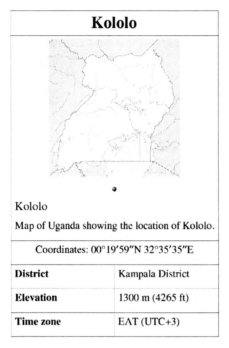 Kololo Map of Uganda showing the location of Kololo.	
Coordinates: 00°19′59″N 32°35′35″E	
District	Kampala District
Elevation	1300 m (4265 ft)
Time zone	EAT (UTC+3)

Kololo is a hill in Kampala, the largest city and capital of Uganda.

Location

Kololo is close to the centre of Kampala, bordered by Naguru to the east, Bukoto to the north, Mulago to the northwest, Makerere to the west, Nakasero to the southwest and Kibuli to the south.

Overview

Starting in the 1950's, before Uganda's Independence, Kololo has been an upscale residential area, due to its central location in the city and to the spectacular views that the hill offers. Kololo is a popular location for Diplomatic Missions to Uganda, housing more than a dozen Embassies and Ambassadors' residences.

During the 2000's, hotels, banks, hospitals and other corporate entities have begun to infiltrate the hill, mainly to serve the elite who reside there, away from the noise and traffic congestion in the central business district located on the neighbouring hill called Nakasero.

At the summit of the hill, there are television and telecommunication masts.

Landmarks

Landmarks on Kololo Hill or near the hill include:

- A branch of DFCU Bank
- Arya Sumaj School
- Casino Simba
- Centenary Park
- Dr. Stockley's Hospital
- East Kololo Primary School
- Embassy of Algeria
- Embassy of the People's Republic of China
- Embassy of the Democratic Republic of Congo
- Embassy of Egypt
- Embassy of Germany
- Embassy of Libya
- Embassy of North Korea
- Embassy of Russia
- Embassy of Rwanda
- Embassy of Saudi Arabia
- Embassy of South Africa
- Garden City Mall
- Hotel Africana
- Independence Park
- Jinja Road Police Station
- Kampala Christian Cemetery
- Kampala Golf Course
- Kampala Golf Club
- Kampala Hospital Limited
- Kampala Airport
- Kampala Protea Hotel
- Kitante High School
- Kololo Secondary School
- Kololo Hospital
- Lincoln International School
- Metropole Hotel
- Oasis Mall
- Speke Apartments
- Uganda Management Institute

- Uganda National Museum
- Zain Telecommunications Headquarters
- The headquarters of Opportunity Uganda Limited, a Tier II Financial Institution

External links

- About Kololo [1]

Photos

- Photo of Kololo Hill [2]

See also

- Kampala
- Nakasero
- Mulago
- Kabalagala
- Muyenga
- Mengo

References

Geographical coordinates: 0°19′59″N 32°35′35″E

Uganda Museum

Uganda Museum	
Established	1908
Location	Kampala, Uganda
Website	[1]

The **Uganda Museum** is a museum in Kampala, Uganda, which displays and exhibits ethnological, natural-historical and traditional life collections of Uganda's cultural heritage. The museum was founded in 1908 after George Wilson called for "all articles of interest" on Uganda to be procured.

Also among the collections in the Uganda Museum are playable musical instruments, hunting equipment, weaponry, archaeology and entomology.

Uganda National Cultural Centre

The **Uganda National Cultural Centre** (UNCC) is a Ugandan statutory body that was established by the Uganda National Cultural Centre Act, a 1959 Act of Parliament (amended 1965). Officially inaugurated on 2 December 1959, it is charged with:

- providing and establishing theatres and cultural centres in the country.
- encouraging and developing cultural and artistic activities.
- providing a home to societies, groups and organisations that deal in art,culture and entertainment.

Facilities

The Centre has two main components: the **National Theatre** and the **Nommo Gallery**, both of which are located in central Kampala. The National Theatre provides a venue for stage performances of different kinds, and also serves as a cinema; the Nommo Gallery features exhibitions of works of art by both Ugandan and foreign artists. The Centre also offers a snack bar, which claims to offer the "best African dishes served with best spices and ambience", and the Craft Village, where locally made handicrafts are sold.

Management

Oversight of the UNCC is the responsibility of an eight-member Board of Trustees, appointed by the Minister of Gender, Labour and Social Development. The Board then appoints a management team and hires other employees.

External links

Phone: +256 (0) 41 425 4567 Homepage: http://ugandanationalculturalcentre.org/

Nakasero Market

Nakasero Market is a market in Kampala, Uganda, located at the foot of Nakasero hill. It sells fresh food, textiles, shoes and cheap electronics.

References

- Uganda Travel Guide [1]

Port Bell

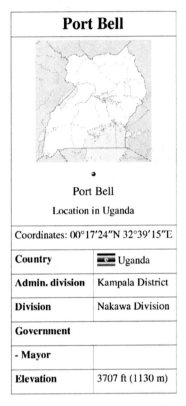

Port Bell	
Location in Uganda	
Coordinates: 00°17′24″N 32°39′15″E	
Country	🇺🇬 Uganda
Admin. division	Kampala District
Division	Nakawa Division
Government	
- Mayor	
Elevation	3707 ft (1130 m)

Port Bell is a small industrial centre in the greater metropolitan Kampala area, in Uganda. Port Bell has a rail link and a rail/road ferry wharf used for International traffic across Lake Victoria to Tanzania and Kenya.

Location

It is located at the end of a narrow inlet of Lake Victoria, approximately 7 miles (11 km), by road, southeast of the central business district of Kampala. The coordinates of Port Bell are:00 17 24N, 32 39 15E (Latitude:0.2900; Longitude:32.6540).

Overview

The port is named after Sir Hesketh Bell, a British commissioner, who took over administration of Britain's interests in Uganda in 1906. Its rail link is a branch line from the Kampala-Jinja main line.

Lake Victoria ferries operate from Port Bell linking Kampala to other railhead ports on Lake Victoria including Jinja, Kisumu and Mwanza. The Port Bell ferry wharf is visible on high-resolution Google

Earth photos at latitude 0.2885° longitude 32.653°. A ferry is shown loading truck and rail coaches while another waits.

When the first stage of the Uganda Railway was completed in 1901, the railhead was at Kisumu, 12 hours journey from Port Bell by ship. Ferries brought goods by lake between Port Bell and Kisumu. It was not until 1931 that a branch line of the railway from Nakuru reached Kampala and then Port Bell.

Industry

At present, Uganda Breweries has its main brewery at Port Bell. In the 1960s one of the first instant tea factories was located at Port Bell as was a factory distilling Waragi, a distilled alcoholic beverage.

Landmarks

The landmarks in or near Port Bell include:

- Luzira Maximum Security Prison - Has a capacity of 20,000 inmates including about 500 on death row
- Quality Chemical Industries Limited ARV Factory - The US$40 million factory is the only one in sub-Saharan Africa that manufactures triple ARV therapy medication.
- Uganda Breweries Limited - A division of East African Breweries and maker of Uganda Waragi, a tripple-distilled gin.
- Port Bell - The port, located on the shores of Lake Nalubaale, handles both passenger and cargo traffic destined for Kisumu, Kenya and Mwanza and Musoma in Tanzania.

Air travel

Before the jet airline era, Port Bell was a landing point on the Imperial Airways flying boat passenger and mail route from Southampton to Johannesburg's Vaal Dam. Port Bell linked Khartoum and Kisumu. The nearby Silver Springs hotel was originally built by BOAC as a rest stop for passengers between long flights.

External links

- About Port Bell in 2009 [1]

See also

- Railway stations in Uganda
- Transport in Uganda

External links

- MSN Map - elevation = 1132m [2]

Geographical coordinates: 00°17′24″N 32°39′15″E

Lubiri

Lubiri (or **Mengo Palace**) is the royal compound of the Kabaka or king of Buganda, located in Mengo, a suburb of Kampala, the Ugandan capital. The original Lubiri was destroyed in the May 1966 Battle of Mengo Hill, at the culmination of the struggle between Mutesa II and Milton Obote for power.

Things to Do and See in Other Parts of Uganda

Lake Albert (Africa)

Lake Albert	
 2002 NASA MODIS satellite picture. The dotted grey line is the border between Congo (DRC) (left) and Uganda (right).	
Coordinates	1°41′N 30°55′E
Primary inflows	Victoria Nile
Primary outflows	Albert Nile
Basin countries	Democratic Republic of Congo, Uganda
Max. length	160 km
Max. width	30 km
Surface area	5,300 km² (2,046 sq. mi.)
Average depth	25 m
Max. depth	58 m
Water volume	132 km³
Surface elevation	615 m
Settlements	Butiaba, Pakwach
References	

Lake Albert − also **Albert Nyanza** and formerly **Lake Mobutu Sese Seko** − is one of the African Great Lakes. It is Africa's seventh largest lake, and ranks as the world's twenty-seventh largest lake by volume.

Geography

Lake Albert is located in the center of the continent, on the border between Uganda and the Democratic Republic of the Congo (formerly Zaire). Lake Albert is the northernmost of the chain of lakes in the Great Rift Valley; it is about 160 km (100 mi) long and 30 km (19 mi) wide, with a maximum depth of 51 m (168 ft), and a surface elevation of 619 m (2,030 ft) above sea level.

Lake Albert is part of the complicated system of the upper Nile. Its main sources are the Victoria Nile, ultimately coming from Lake Victoria to the southeast, and the Semliki River, which issues from Lake Edward to the southwest. The water of the Victoria Nile is much less saline than that of Lake Albert. Its outlet, at the northernmost tip of the lake, is the Albert Nile (which becomes known as the Mountain Nile when it enters Sudan).

Rivers and lakes of Uganda. Click image to enlarge.

At the southern end of the lake, where the Semliki comes in, there are swamps. Farther south loom the mighty Ruwenzori Range, while a range of hills called the Blue Mountains tower over the northwestern shore. The few settlements along the shore include Butiaba and Pakwach.

History

In 1864, when the explorer Samuel Baker found the lake; he named it after the recently deceased Prince Albert, consort of Queen Victoria. Congolese president Mobutu Sese Seko temporarily named the lake after himself.

Heritage Oil and Tullow Oil have announced major oil finds in the Lake Albert basin, with estimates that the multi-billion barrel field will prove to be the largest onshore field found in sub-saharan Africa for over twenty years.

See also

- Energy in Uganda

References

- Food and Agriculture Organization of the United Nations [1]
- World Lakes Database entry for Lake Albert [2]

Entebbe

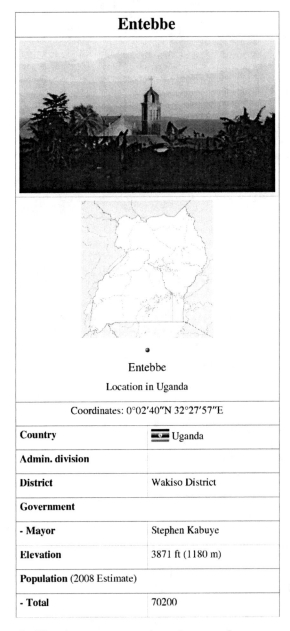

Entebbe	
Location in Uganda	
Coordinates: 0°02′40″N 32°27′57″E	
Country	Uganda
Admin. division	
District	Wakiso District
Government	
- Mayor	Stephen Kabuye
Elevation	3871 ft (1180 m)
Population (2008 Estimate)	
- Total	70200

Entebbe is a city in Uganda. The city was, at one time, the seat of government for the Protectorate of Uganda, prior to Independence in 1962. Entebbe is the location of Entebbe International Airport, Uganda's largest commercial and military airport, best known for the dramatic rescue of 100 hostages kidnapped by terrorists of the PFLP and Revolutionary Cells (RZ) organizations.

Location

Entebbe sits on the northern shores of Lake Victoria, Africa's largest lake. Entebbe lies at 00.04N, 32.465E. It is situated in Wakiso District, approximately 37 kilometres (23 mi), southwest of Kampala, Uganda's largest city and capital.

The Municipality is located on a peninsula into Lake Victoria covering a total area of 56.2 square kilometres (21.7 sq mi), out of which 20 square kilometres (7.7 sq mi) is water.

Population

During the 2002 national census, Entebbe's population was estimated at 55,086 people. In 2008, the Uganda Bureau of Statistics estimated the population of the town at 70,200.

History

"Entebbe", in the local Luganda language, means a "seat", and was probably named that because it was the place where a Baganda chief sat to adjudicate legal cases. It first became a British colonial administrative and commercial centre in 1893 when Sir Gerald Portal, a colonial Commissioner, used it as a base. Port Bell went on to become Kampala's harbour. Although no ships dock there now, there is still a jetty, which was used by Lake Victoria ferries. Entebbe is perhaps best known to Europeans as the home of Entebbe International Airport, the main international airport of Uganda, which was started in 1947. The Entebbe airport was the scene of one of the most daring counter-terrorism operations in history when soldiers from an elite unit of the Israeli army freed over 100 hostages following a hijacking by a group of Palestinian and German terrorists. It was also from this airport that Queen Elizabeth II departed Africa to return to England in 1952 when learning of her father's death and that she had become Queen.

Tourist Attractions

- The extensive National Botanical Gardens, laid out in 1898, are located in Entebbe.
- Entebbe is the home of the Uganda Virus Research Institute (UVRI).
- Entebbe is the location of the Uganda Wildlife Education Center (UWEC) The Center also serves as the national zoo. The entrance to the Center is located near the jetty. Foreign visitors have noted the seeming incongruity of wild monkeys sitting in the trees over the Center's paths.
- Entebbe is the location of Nkumba University, one of the thirty one (31) licensed institutions of tertiary education in Uganda.
- Entebbe is also the location of State House, the official residence of the President of Uganda

Sunset over Entebbe

Entebbe International Airport

Bugonga Church in Entebbe

Entebbe sits on the northern shores of Lake Victoria

Other Landmarks

Landmarks within the city limits or close to its edges include:

- The offices of Entebbe City Council
- Three branches of Barclays Bank
- A branch of Ecobank
- A branch of Equity Bank
- Two branches of Orient Bank
- A branch of PostBank Uganda
- Two branches of Stanbic Bank
- A branch of Bank of Africa
- A branch of Uganda Finance Trust Limited - A Tier III Financial Institution

Climate

Entebbe features a tropical rainforest climate with relatively constant temperatures throughout the course of the year. Entebbe has noticeably wetter and drier months, with January being the city's driest month and a noticeably drier stretch from July through September. However, since average monthly precipitation in each of these months is above 60 mm, Entebbe has no true dry season and therefore falls under the tropical rainforest climate category. Entebbe's wettest months are April and May, when, on average, roughly 250 mm of rain falls in each of these months. Entebbe's average annual temperature is approximately 21 degrees Celsius.

Climate data for Entebbe													
Month	Jan	Feb	Mar	Apr	May	Jun	Jul	Aug	Sep	Oct	Nov	Dec	Year
Record high °C (°F)	32 (90)	32 (90)	33 (91)	28 (82)	28 (82)	29 (84)	28 (82)	29 (84)	31 (88)	29 (84)	32 (90)	29 (84)	33 (91)
Average high °C (°F)	27 (81)	27 (81)	26 (79)	26 (79)	25 (77)	25 (77)	24 (75)	25 (77)	26 (79)	26 (79)	26 (79)	26 (79)	25.6 (78.1)
Average low °C (°F)	18 (64)	18 (64)	18 (64)	18 (64)	18 (64)	17 (63)	17 (63)	17 (63)	17 (63)	17 (63)	18 (64)	17 (63)	17.5 (63.5)
Record low °C (°F)	14 (57)	14 (57)	14 (57)	15 (59)	15 (59)	14 (57)	12 (54)	13 (55)	14 (57)	14 (57)	14 (57)	14 (57)	12 (54)
Precipitation mm (inches)	66 (2.6)	91 (3.58)	160 (6.3)	257 (10.12)	244 (9.61)	122 (4.8)	76 (2.99)	74 (2.91)	74 (2.91)	94 (3.7)	132 (5.2)	117 (4.61)	1507 (59.33)
Source: BBC Weather													

See also

- Operation Entebbe
- Entebbe Airport

References

Geographical coordinates: 00°02′40″N 32°27′57″E

Rwenzori Mountains

The **Rwenzori Mountains**, previously called the **Ruwenzori Range** (the spelling having been changed in about 1980 to conform more closely with the local name) is a mountain range of central Africa, often referred to as Mt. Rwenzori, located on the border between Uganda and the DRC, with heights of up to 5,109 m (16,761 ft) at 0°23′09″N 29°52′18″E. The highest Rwenzoris are permanently snow-capped, and they, along with Mount Kilimanjaro and Mount Kenya are the only such in Africa.[*citation needed*]

Rwenzori Range

Geologic history

The mountains formed about three million years ago in the late Pliocene as a result of an uplifted block of crystalline rocks such as: gneiss, amphibolite granite and quartzite, "pushed up by tremendous forces originating deep within the earth's crust". This uplift divided the paleolake Obweruka and created two of the present-day African Great Lakes: Albert and Edward and George on the flanks of the Albertine (western) Rift of the East African Rift, the African part of the Great Rift Valley.

Margherita Peak on Mount Stanley is the highest point in the range

The range is about 120 km (75 mi) long and 65 km (40 mi) wide. It consists of six massifs separated by deep gorges: Mount Stanley (5,109m), Mount Speke (4,890m), Mount Baker (4,843m), Mount Emin (4,798m), Mount Gessi (4,715m) and Mount Luigi di Savoia (4,627m). Mount Stanley is the largest and has several subsidiary summits, with Margherita Peak being the highest point. The rock is metamorphic, and the mountains are believed to have been tilted and squeezed upwards by plate movement. They are in an extremely humid area, and frequently enveloped in clouds.

Human history

The Rwenzori range is the home of the Konjo and Amba peoples. In the early 1900s, these two tribes were added to the Toro Kingdom by the colonial powers. The Konjo and Amba agitated for separation from Toro beginning in the 1950s, a movement that became an armed secessionist movement, known as Rwenzururu, by the mid-1960s. The insurgency ended through a negotiated settlement in 1982, though the Rwenzururu Kingdom was acknowledged by the government in 2008.

House and people in Kasese District, Uganda

The first modern European sighting of the Rwenzori was by the expedition of Henry Morton Stanley in 1889 (the aforementioned clouds are considered to explain why two decades of previous explorers had not seen them). On June 7, the expedition's second-in-command and its military commander, William Grant Stairs, climbed to 10,677 feet, the first known non-African ever to climb in the range. The first ascent to the summit was made by the Duke of the Abruzzi in 1906.

Flora and fauna

The Rwenzori are known for their vegetation, ranging from tropical rainforest through alpine meadows to snow; and for their animal population, including forest elephants, several primate species and many endemic birds. The range supports its own species and varieties of Giant groundsel and Giant lobelia and even has a six metre high heather covered in moss that lives on one of its peaks. Most of the range is now a World Heritage Site and is covered jointly by The Rwenzori Mountains National Park in Uganda and the Parc National des Virunga in Congo.

Lower Bigo Bog at 3400m in the Rwenzori Mountains with giant lobelia in foreground

Vegetation zones

> There are 5 different Vegetation Zones found in the Rwenzori Mountains. These are grassland (1000–2000m), montane forest (2000–3000m), bamboo/mimulopsis zone (2500–3500m), Heather/Rapanea zone (3000–4000m) and the afro-alpine moorland zone (4000–4500m). At higher altitudes some plants reach an unusually large size, such as lobelia and groundsels. The vegetation in the Rwenzori Mountains is unique to equatorial alpine Africa.

Flora vs altitude

Meters / Order	1500	2000	2500	3000	3200	3400	3600	3800	4000	4200	4400	4600	4800	5000	5100
Lamiales			*Mimulopsis elliotii* *Mimulopsis arborescens*												
Rosales	*Prunus africana*			*Hagenia abyssinica*											
									Alchemilla subnivalis *Alchemilla stuhlmanii* *Alchemilla triphylla* *Alchemilla johnstonii*						
						Alchemilla argyrophylla									
Fabales		*Albizia gummifera*													
Cornales		*Alangium chinense*													
Malpighiales	*Casearia battiscombei* *Croton macrostachyus* *Neoboutonia macrocalyx* *Symphonia globulifera*					*Hypericum* sp									
					Hypericum revolutum *Hypericum bequaertii*										
Asparagales			*Scadoxus cyrtanthiflorus*												
					Disa stairsii										
Asterales						*Dendrosenecio erici-rosenii*									
					Dendrosenecio adnivalis *Helichrysum* sp. *Lobelia bequaertii* *Lobelia wollastonii*				*Helichchrysum guilelmii*						
										Helichchrysum stuhlmanii					
									Senecio transmarinus *Senecio mattirolii*						
Apiales									*Peucedanum kerstenii*						
Myrtales	*Syzygium guineense*														

Order	1500	2000	2500	3000	3200	3400	3600	3800	4000	4200	4400	4600	4800	5000	5100
Sapindales	*Allophylus abyssinicus*														
Gentianales	*Tabernaemontana sp.*							*Galium ruwenzoriense*							
Ericales	*Pouteria adolfi-friedericii*				*Erica arborea* *Erica trimera*										
				Erica silvatica *Erica johnstonii*											
Brassicales								*Subularia monticola*							
Primulales			*Rapanea rhododendroides*												
Ranunculales								*Ranunculus oreophytus* *Arabis alpina*							
Santalales	*Strombosia scheffleri*														
Poales			*Yushania alpina*					*Carex runssoroensis* *Festuca abyssinica*							
											Poa ruwenzoriensis				
Lecanorales						*Usnea*									
Order Meters	1500	2000	2500	3000	3200	3400	3600	3800	4000	4200	4400	4600	4800	5000	5100

Sources:

Glacial recession in Rwenzori

Main article: Retreat of glaciers since 1850#Tropical glaciers

A subject of concern in recent years has been the impact of climate change on Rwenzori's glaciers. In 1906 the Rwenzori had 43 named glaciers distributed over 6 mountains with a total area of 7.5 km²., about half the total glacier area in Africa. By 2005, less than half of these survive, on only 3 mountains, with an area of about 1.5 km². Recent scientific studies such as those by Dr Richard Taylor of University College London have attributed this to global climate change, and investigated its impact on the mountain's vegetation and biodiversity. In general, though, glacier growth and recedence are not necessarily tied to trends in temperatures as much as trends in precipitation.

Ornithologist James P. Chapin on a Rwenzori expedition, 1925

References

- *Glaciers of the Middle East and Africa*, Williams, Richard S., Jr. (editor) In: U. S. Geological Survey Professional Paper, 1991, pp.G1-G70
- *Guide to the Ruwenzori*, Osmaston,H.A., Pasteur,D. 1972, Mountain Club of Uganda. 200 p.
- *Recession of Equatorial Glaciers. A Photo Documentation* [1], Hastenrath, S., 2008, Sundog Publishing, Madison, WI, ISBN 978-0-9729033-3-2, 144 pp.
- *Tropical Glaciers*, Kaser, G., Osmaston, H.A. 2002, Cambridge University Press, UK. 207 p.
- *Ruwenzori*, de Filippi, F. 1909. Constable, London. 408 p.
- Greenpeace article "The Death of the Ice Gigantaurs" [2]
- BBC Article "Fabled ice field set to vanish" [3]
- Dr Taylor's Homepage, with information about the impact of climate change on Rwenzori. [4]
- Kaser et al. 2006, in *International Book of Climatology* 24: 329–339 (2004)

External links

- Rwenzori Mountains Historical Climbing and Centenary Celebrations [5]
- rwenzori.com - Rwenzori Mountains tourist information and tips [6]
- Account and photos of a climb up the Ruwenzoris (Congo side) [7]
- 30 photos of a climb up the Ruwenzoris (Congo side) [8]
- Account and planning logistics of a climb up the Rwenzoris (Congo side) [9]
- The remarkable plants and animals of the Ruwenzoris [10]
- Gallery of pictures [11]

Toro Kingdom

Flag of Toro

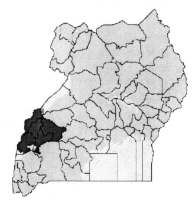

Original Kingdom of Toro and its districts

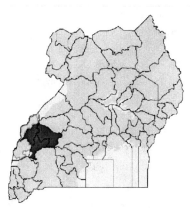

Kingdom of Toro since 1993

Toro is one of the four traditional kingdoms located within the borders of Uganda. It was founded in 1830 when Omukama Kaboyo Olimi I, the eldest son of Omukama Nyamutukura Kyebambe III of Bunyoro, rebelled and established his own independent kingdom. Incorporated back into Bunyoro-Kitara in 1876, it reasserted its independence in 1891.

Like Buganda, Bunyoro, and Busoga, Toro's monarchy was abolished in 1967 by the government of Uganda, but was reinstated in 1993. The incumbent monarch is King Rukiraba Saija Oyo Nyimba Kabamba Iguru Rukidi IV.

Abakama of Toro

The following is a list of the *Abakama* of Toro, starting around 1800 AD:

1. Olimi I: 1822 - 1865
2. Ruhaga of Toro: 1865 - 1866
3. Nyaika Kyebambe I: 1866 - 1871 and 1871 - 1872
4. Rukidi I: 1871 - 1871
5. Olimi II: 1872 - 1875
6. Rukidi II: 1875 - 1875
7. Rububi Kyebambe II: 1875 and 1877 - 1879
8. Kakende Nyamuyonjo: 1875 - 1876 and 1879 - 1880
9. Katera: 1876 - 1877 Followed by Interregnum, reverted to Bunyoro:1880 - 1891
10. Kyebambe III: 1891 - 1928
11. Rukidi III: 1929 - 1965
12. Olimi III: 1965 - 1995. Interrupted by Interregnum: 1967 - 1993
13. Rukidi IV: 1995 - Present

External links

- Toro Kingdom [1]

See also

- Omukama of Toro
- Kingdom of Buganda

[2]

Bibliography

- Ingham, Kenneth. *The Kingdom of Toro in Uganda*. London: Methuen, 1975.

Ankole

For the breed of cattle, see Ankole-Watusi (cattle).

Ankole, also referred to as **Nkore**, is one of four traditional kingdoms in Uganda. The kingdom is located in the southwestern Uganda, east of Lake Edward. It was ruled by a monarch known as The Mugabe or Omugabe of Ankole. The kingdom was formally abolished in 1967 by the government of President Milton Obote, and is still not officially restored. The people of Ankole are called **Banyankole** (singular: **Munyankole**) in Runyankole language, a Bantu language.

On October 25, 1901, the Kingdom of Nkore was incorporated into the British protectorate of Uganda by the signing of the Ankole agreement.

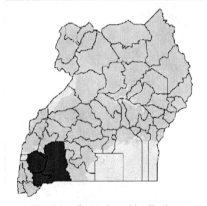

Kingdom of Ankole and its districts

Due to the rearranging of the country by Idi Amin, Ankole no longer exist as an administrative unit. It is divided into six districts: Bushenyi District, Ntungamo District, Mbarara District, Kiruhura District, Ibanda District and Isingiro District.

History of pre-colonial ethnic relations in Ankole

State flag of the Kingdom of Ankole

The pastoralist Hima (also known as Bahima) established dominion over the agricultural Iru (also known as Bairu) some time before the nineteenth century. The Hima and Iru established close relations based on trade and symbolic recognition, but they were unequal partners in these relations. The Iru were legally and socially inferior to the Hima, and the symbol of this inequality was cattle, which only the Hima could own. The two groups retained their separate identities through rules prohibiting intermarriage and, when such marriages occurred, making them invalid.

The Hima provided cattle products that otherwise would not have been available to Iru farmers. Because the Hima population was much smaller than the Iru population, gifts and tribute demanded by the Hima could be supplied fairly easily. These factors probably made Hima-Iru relations tolerable, but they were nonetheless reinforced by the superior military organization and training of the Hima.

The kingdom of Ankole expanded by annexing territory to the south and east. In many cases, conquered herders were incorporated into the dominant Hima stratum of society, and agricultural populations were adopted as Iru or slaves and treated as legal inferiors. Neither group could own cattle, and slaves could not herd cattle owned by the Hima.

Ankole society evolved into a system of ranked statuses, where even among the cattle-owning elite, patron-client ties were important in maintaining social order. Men gave cattle to the king (mugabe) to demonstrate their loyalty and to mark life-cycle changes or victories in cattle raiding. This loyalty was often tested by the king's demands for cattle or for military service. In return for homage and military service, a man received protection from the king, both from external enemies and from factional disputes with other cattle owners.

The mugabe authorized his most powerful chiefs to recruit and lead armies on his behalf, and these warrior bands were charged with protecting Ankole borders. Only Hima men could serve in the army, however, and the prohibition on Iru military training almost eliminated the threat of Iru rebellion. Iru legal inferiority was also symbolized in the legal prohibition against Iru owning cattle. And, because marriages were legitimized through the exchange of cattle, this prohibition helped reinforce the ban on Hima-Iru intermarriage. The Iru were also denied highlevel political appointments, although they were often appointed to assist local administrators in Iru villages.

The Iru had a number of ways to redress grievances against Hima overlords, despite their legal inferiority. Iru men could petition the king to end unfair treatment by a Hima patron. Iru people could not be subjugated to Hima cattle-owners without entering into a patron-client contract.

A number of social pressures worked to destroy Hima domination of Ankole. Miscegenation took place despite prohibitions on intermarriage, and children of these unions (abambari) often demanded their rights as cattle owners, leading to feuding and cattle-raiding. From what is present-day Rwanda, East African Federation , groups launched repeated attacks against the Hima during the nineteenth century. To counteract these pressures, several Hima warlords recruited Iru men into their armies to protect the southern borders of Ankole.

References

⊚ *This article incorporates public domain material from websites or documents* [1] *of the Library of Congress Country Studies.*

External links

- World Statesmen - Uganda [1]
- A tour guide to Ankole Culture - Uganda [2]
- Historical map of Ankole [3]

pnb:انکول

Busoga

Busoga is a traditional Bantu kingdom in present-day Uganda.

It is a cultural institution that promotes popular participation and unity among the people of Busoga, through cultural and developmental programs for the improved livelihood of the people of Busoga. It strives for a united people of Busoga, who enjoy economic, social and cultural prosperity. It also continues to enhance, revamp and pave the way for an efficient institutional and management system for the Kyabazinga kingship.

Busoga, literally translated to *Land of the Soga*, is the kingdom of the 11 principalities of the Basoga/Soga (singular **Musoga**) people. The term Busoga also loosely refers to the area that is generally indigenous to the Basoga. The kingdom's capital is located in Bugembe, which is near Jinja, the second largest city in Uganda. As of June 2007, Busoga Kingdom is composed of seven politically organised districts: Kamuli, Iganga, Bugiri, Mayuge, Jinja, and the newly created districts of Kaliro and Busiki. Each district is headed by democratically elected chairpersons or Local Council Five, while municipalities are headed by an elected mayor. Jinja is the industrial and economical hub of Busoga. The Busoga area is bounded on the north by the swampy Lake Kyoga which separates it from Lango, on the west by the Victoria Nile which separates it from Buganda, on the south by Lake Victoria which separates it from Tanzania and Kenya, and on the east by the Mpologoma River, which separates it from various smaller tribal groups (Padhola, Bugwere, Bugisu, etc). Busoga also includes some islands in Lake Victoria, such as Buvuma Island.

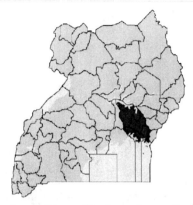

A map of Busoga Kingdom and some of its districts

The Busoga flag

The Kyabazinga

Main articles: Kyabazinga of Busoga and Inhebantu of Busoga

Title of Head of Busoga : His Royal Highness Isebantu Kyabazinga

Short Title : The Kyabazinga of Busoga

Busoga is ruled by the Isebantu Kyabazinga of Busoga. This name was a symbol of unity derived from the expression and recognition by the Basoga that their leader was the "father of all people who brings all of them together", and who also serves as their cultural leader.

Main article: Henry Wako Muloki

In 1995, the government restored monarchies in Uganda with the promulgation of the new constitution of the Republic of Uganda; Article 246(1). On February 11, 1996, His Royal Highness Henry Wako Muloki was reinstated as Kyabazinga Isebantu of Busoga. He served until Monday, 1 September 2008, when he finally succumbed to esophageal cancer at the Mulago National Referral Hospital in Kampala, at the age of 87.

In a condolence message, Y.K Museveni, the president of Uganda described Muloki as "a great cultural leader and father" who was "generous and kind."

Since his re-installation on 11 February 1996, Muloki had been a unifying factor in Busoga, the President noted. "The Government has had the privilege of working with Isebantu Muloki in developing our nation."

Referring to the Kyabazinga as "a strong pillar", Museveni said although Busoga was one of the youngest kingdoms, under the leadership of Muloki, it had become strong.

"Uganda mourns not only one of her esteemed traditional leaders but a national who put development and the welfare of the people of Busoga at the helm of his reign," Museveni added.

The achievements of Muloki include special programmes initiated for girl-child education, for the youth and for the elderly and the disadvantaged.

History of Busoga

Early contact with European explorers

Main articles: Uganda before 1900 and Colonial Uganda

Written history begins for Busoga in the year 1862. On 28 July 1862, John Hanning Speke, an explorer for the Royal Geographical Society, arrived at Ripon Falls, near the site of the modern town of Jinja, where the Victoria Nile spills out of Lake Victoria and begins its descent to Egypt. Since Speke's route inland from the East African coast had taken him around the southern end of the lake Victoria, he approached Busoga from the west through Buganda. Having reached his goal – the source of the Nile, he turned northward and followed the river downstream without further exploring Busoga. He records, however, being told that "Usoga" *(the Swahili form of the name 'Busoga')* was an "island", which indicates that the term meant to surrounding peoples essentially what it means today. The present day Busoga Kingdom was, and still is, bounded on the north by the swampy Lake Kyoga, on the west by the Victoria Nile, on the south by Lake Victoria, and on the east by the Mpologoma River.

Early demographics

Main articles: Uganda before 1900 and Colonial Uganda

In the 19th century, one of the principal routes along which Europeans travelled from the coast to Buganda passed through the southern part of Busoga. From John Speke and James Grant, Sir Gerald Portal, F.D Lugard, J.R. Macdonald, and Bishop Tucket all noted that Busoga was plentifully supplied with food and was densely settled as a result. However, between 1898-99 and 1900-01, the first indications of sleeping sickness were reported.   In 1906, orders were issued to evacuate the region.

Despite the attempts to clear the area, the epidemic continued in force until 1910. As a result, most of the densely populated parts of Busoga, the home land of over 200,000 persons in the 19th Century, was totally cleared of the population in the ten years. Lubas palace at Bukaleba, also the coveted European fruit mission, collapsed and relocated to other parts of Busoga. Southern Busoga constituted of about one third of the land area of Busoga, and, in 1910, southern Busoga was vacant. In the 1920s and 1930s, some of the evacuees who survived the epidemic began to return to their original land. However, in 1940 a new outbreak of sleeping sickness resurfaced in the area, and it was only in 1956 that resettlement, promoted by the government began again, but things were not going to be the same again. Few Basoga returned to their traditional lands.

The consequences of the catastrophe were that the Southern part of Busoga, the area roughly corresponding to what Johnston delimited as the most densely populated area, was virtually uninhabited. Other areas originally affected by sleeping sickness, including the eastern margins of Bukooli and Busiki conties were evidently depopulated too. Famines, too, resulted in substantial population movements. Several areas in north east Busoga and in the adjacent Bukandi district across the Mpologoma river were repeatedly struck by famines in 1898 to 1900, 1907, 1908, 1917, 1918 and 1944. Populations in these areas reduced, many people, falling victims to the famines while the survivors moved to other areas for safety.

The effects of these movements were apparent from the growth in population density in the central area of Busoga and in urban and peri-urban areas of Busoga. Many Basoga left Busoga in the same period, settling in other districts. The demographic profile of Busoga today is, as a consequence of all these developments. Today, Busoga is home to many people, of about 6 different origins.

Early economic status

Main articles: Early independent Uganda and Uganda under Amin

In the pre-colonial era, people left their traditional lands and state structures disappeared. A number of clans and states decimated and people migrated into Busoga in large numbers in this century, carrying with them the traditions and [cultures of other lands. The most important causes of these movements were mainly famines and epidemics, which occurred within and the surrounding areas.

Busoga experienced massive movement of people right from the early period that led to its construction as a nation. Several factors contributed to the trend of events. They included mainly factors ranging from famine and security. Today, these factors continue to affect and define the population mobility in the kingdom, in addition to the quest for employment and social amenities. The changes in the demographical trends have continued to witness a population influx in urban and peri-urban areas of Busoga kingdom for the above reasons. Towns like Jinja, Iganga, Kamuli, Kaliro, and their surrounding areas are some of the areas that continue to face high levels of immigration. Immigrants join town life in search for jobs and security. Between 1920 and the 1970s, Jinja, Busoga's capital city, experienced economic changes and gained in economic importance. During this period, it transformed into an industrial town with the steady high cotton production, as well as the completion of the Uganda Railway and Owen Falls dam. These factors elevated Jinja into an agri-industrial centre with over 46 factories, several cottage industries and a well-developed infrastructure. These developments attracted people in the form of labour from the rural areas of Busoga to work in those factories, help in house keeping or in doing other urban development related activities. Externally, many people also came from the neighbouring areas outside Busoga. Among the new comers were families of Asian origin who came to do business. Estates like Mpumudde and Walukuba were developed to accommodate the increasing population. Other services like piped water, electricity, roads, hospitals and schools were also extended to serve the population. In the villages, the majority of people, with the assured market in towns, concentrated on agriculture. They grew both cash and food crops like cotton, coffee, bananas, potatoes and cassava, fruits and vegetables. Standards of living drastically improved and Busoga kingdom raised its revenue and constructed more infrastructures. It reduced the subsistence farming system of life and turned to real economic production that was in demand by Europeans. By independence in 1962, Busoga was one of the most powerful regions in Uganda. Its power lay in the regional capital, Jinja which is Uganda's second largest city. Jinja was the home to 70% of Uganda's industries and also hosted the Nalubaale Power Station (Owen Falls Dam) that supplies electricity to Uganda and parts of Kenya and Tanzania. Jinja was also the home of the majority of Uganda's Asian population. The Ugandan Asians, who had been brought to Uganda from the Indian sub-continent by the British during colonial times, had helped to establish Jinja as one of East Africa's most vibrant commercial centres.

Early political status

Main article: Uganda before 1900

About the turn of the 16th century, an important event took place, which was to give the Basoga their peculiar cultural configuration. This was the advent of the Baisengobi clan, who bear their historical descendancy from Bunyoro. Prince Mukama Namutukula from the royal family (Babiito) of Bunyoro is said to have left Bunyoro around the 16th century and as part of Bunyoro's expansionist policy and trekked eastwards across Lake Kyoga with his wife Nawudo, a handful of servants, arms and a dog, and landed at Iyingo, located at the northern point of Busoga in the present day Kamuli District.

Prince Mukama loved hunting and his adventures exposed him to the beauties of the new found land. For sometime he engaged himself in blacksmithing, making hoes, iron utensils and spears. Prince Mukama and wife Nawudo bore several children of whom only five boys survived. On his departure back to Bunyoro, Prince Mukama allocated them areas within his influence as overseers. In this way, the first-born Wakoli was given to oversee the area called Bukooli, Zibondo was to administer Bulamogi, Ngobi was given Kigulu, Tabingwa was to oversee Luuka, while the youngest son Kitimbo was to settle in Bugabula. These loosely allotted areas of supervision to the Prince's sons were later to become major administrative and centers cultural authority in Busoga. With time passing without the expected return of their father, the five sons of Prince Mukama regarded themselves as the legitimate rulers over their respective areas by virtue of their family origin (Babiito). They continued to preside over their respective dominions; employing governing methods and cultural rituals like those from Bunyoro-Kitara. This state of affairs in Busoga's political and cultural arrangement continued till the late 19th century when the colonialists persuaded the rulers of Busoga into some form of federation. This federation resulted into a regional Busoga council called Busoga Lukiiko.

Before 1906, although it was often called a 'Kingdom', it was debatable whether Busoga could really be classified as such. Unlike its western neighbor, Buganda, Busoga did not have a central 'all-powerful' figurehead (King or Queen) until 1906, at the behest of the British colonial powers. Prior to this, the Basoga were organized in semi-autonomous chiefdoms, partly under the influence of Bunyoro initially, and then later on, under the partial influence of Buganda.

Main article: Colonial Uganda

Before the coming of the British to Uganda, there was no uniting leadership in Busoga. When Uganda became a British protectorate, attempts were made to create a central form of administration on the model of Buganda which was a fully fledged kingdom. The Buganda King – the Kabaka had lineage going back centuries. However, in Busoga some of the chiefs had been simply appointed by the Kabaka – and it is believed that in some cases they were descendants of favored Baganda chiefs who were given authority to rule over land in Busoga. Others simply belonged to powerful landowning families in Busoga that had become self-appointed rulers over vast areas. The British brought all these chiefs into an administrative structure called the Lukiiko. The British appointed a Muganda from Buganda, Semei Kakungulu as the President of the Lukiiko and he became Busoga's first leader, although the British refused to give him the title of 'King', as they did not regard him as a real king.

However wrangles amongst the different chiefs and clans continued, and most Basoga still retained affiliation to their chief, clan or dialect. It was also not helpful that the 'King' was from Buganda. The Lukiiko structure collapsed. The structure had however given the Basoga a taste of what influence they could muster in the protectorate if they had a King. It would elevate them to the level of Bunyoro and Buganda.

Meanwhile, the white colonial rulers were grooming Chief Yosia Nadiope, the Gabula of Bugabula to become the first permanent resident ruler of the formed Busoga federation. Nadiope had been one of the first Basoga students to study at Kings College Budo in 1906. However, catastrophe struck Busoga in 1913, when Nadiope died of malaria. The following year 1914, Chief Ezekeriel Tenywa Wako, the Zibondo of Bulamogi was completing his studies at Kings College Budo. With the support of the British coupled with his background as a Prince, Zibondo of Bulamogi, with his good educational background, was a suitable candidate for the top post. In 1919, the hereditary saza chiefs of Busoga resolved in the Lukiiko to elect Ezekerial Tenywa Wako as president of Busoga. Chief Gideon Obodha of Kigulu, a contending candidate for the post was not familiar with the British system, while William Wilberforce Nadiope Kadhumbula of Bugabula was still an infant. His regent Mwami Mutekanga was a 'mukoopi' (a commoner) who couldn't run for the post. Eventually, in 1918-9, the title of Isebantu Kyabazinga was created and one of the chiefs, Wako took the throne. He was given a salary of 550 pounds, and permitted to collect taxes in Butembe county in lieu of the lost role in his traditional chiefdom of Bulamogi. In 1925, Ezekiel Tenywa Wako, the Kyabazinga of Busoga became a member of Uganda Kings Council, consisting of the Kyabazinga of Busoga, Kabaka of Buganda, the Omukama of Bunyoro, Omukama of Toro/Omukama of Tooro and Omugabe of Ankole.

On 11 February 1939 Owekitibwa Ezekerial Tenywa Wako (late father of the last Isebantu Kyabazinga wa Busoga, HRH Henry Wako Muloki), the Zibondo of Bulamogi was installed as the first Isebantu Kyabazinga wa Busoga which title he continued to hold until 1949 when he retired due to old age. By the time Owekitibwa E.T. Wako retired as the Isebantu Kyabazinga wa Busoga, the Busoga Lukiiko had expanded to include people other than the Hereditary Rulers. These members of the Busoga Lukiiko were elected representatives – two from each of the then 55 Sub-counties in Busoga.

When Owekitibwa E.T.Wako retired, it was necessary to replace him. The Busoga Lukiiko resolved then that the Isebantu Kyabazinga wa Busoga shall always be elected among the five lineages of Baise Ngobi (Ababiito) hereditary rulers – traditionally believed to have been the five sons of Omukama of Bunyoro who immigrated to Busoga from Bunyoro, namely:

Zibondo of Bulamogi Gabula of Bugabula Ngobi of Kigulu Tabingwa of Luuka Nkono of Bukono

This method of election was used for the subsequent elections of the Isebantu Kyabazinga wa Busoga, beginning 1949 when Owekitibwa Chief William Wilberforce Nadiope Kadhumbula of Bugabula was elected Isebantu Kyabazinga wa Busoga for two terms of three years each, followed by Owekitibwa Henry Wako Muloki who also served two terms.

In 1957, the title Inhebantu was introduced as a description of the wife of the Isebantu. This epitomised the gradual unification of Busoga and the evolution of Obwa Kyabazinga bwa Busoga.

When monarchies were abolished in 1966, the Kyabazinga was dethroned. When the dictator Idi Amin expelled the Asians from Uganda in 1972, Jinja suffered both socially and economically. The government of Yoweri Museveni has tried to encourage Ugandan Asians to return. This has helped but has not revitalized Jinja to its former glory. However the Asian influence remains, particularly in the architecture and street names.

Main article: Uganda since 1979

In 1995, the government restored monarchies in Uganda with the promulgation of the new constitution of the Republic of Uganda; Article 246(1). On February 11, 1995, H.R.H Henry Wako Muloki was reinstated as Kyabazinga Isebantu of Busoga, according to Kisoga traditions and culture. Unlike most monarchies, the Kyabazinga has no heir or Crown Prince. Instead, the Kyabazinga is succeeded by a reigning chief elected by the Lukiiko and the Royal Council.

Past Kyabazingas

Obwa Kyabazinga bwa Busoga has evolved over years and each Kyabazinga that has presided over Busoga has added a piece to the process. To date, there have been three past Kyabazingas who have presided over Busoga since 1939 as an established federated state of Busoga.

These have been:- **Chief Ezekiel Tenywa Wako**, who was the first Kyabazinga of Busoga and ascended to the throne in 1939: Yosia Nadiope, and Sir William Wilberforce Nadiope Kadhumbula.

Sir William Wilberforce Kadhumbula succeeded his late father's (Yosia Nadiope) quick sense of judgement and love for the people. He ridded the kingdom of insecurity; eliminating bad elements in society in the famous operation named 'Emizindula,' *(war against theft)*, ended the British policy on the fight against smallpox *(Kawumpuli)*, during which residents were ordered to carry rat tails to Busoga square for counting as evidence that they had really killed the diseases agents (rats). This, he saw as a dehumanising act and joined his subjects to denounce the policy, which brought him in conflict with the British administration. As a result he was exiled to Bunyoro where he was called to lead the Basoga into the Second World War.

His war skills and mobilisation ability earned him Queen Elizabeth's admiration and love. He was honoured with the title Sir among other awards.

He also played a big role in Uganda's independence struggle and before the end of his career, he had served as the first Vice President of the independent Uganda. He was also the Chairman of Uganda People's Congress political party (UPC).

He mobilised for the construction of infrastructures like roads, hospitals, government centres like county and sub-county headquarters and most of all mobilising the Basoga to productive farming of both food and crops.

During his tenure of office doubling as the Vice President, Kyabazinga and UPC Chairman, he managed to push for several development projects in Busoga that include construction of schools like the Balangira High School, which later became Busoga College Mwiri.

Current political setup

Busoga Kingdom Royal Council is composed of the 11 traditional leaders of the 11 traditional chiefdoms of Busoga. They include the five princes and heads of the five royal families of Busoga and the six chiefs of the traditional chiefdoms. They are;

Busoga Kingdom Royal Council

Title	Ssaza (principality or chiefdom)	Head
Zibondo	Bulamogi	Prince G. W Napeera
Gabula	Bugabula	Prince William Nadiope
Ngobi	Kigulu	Prince Izimba Golologolo
Tabingwa	Luuka	Prince W. Tabingwa Nabwana
Nkono	Bukono	Prince C. J. Mutyaba Nkono
Wakooli	Bukooli	Chief David Muluuya Kawunye
Ntembe	Butembe	Chief Badru Waguma
Menya	Bugweri	Chief Kakaire Fred Menya
Kisiki	Busiki	Chief Yekosofato Kawanguzi
Luba	Bunya	Chief Juma Munulo
Nanyumba	Bunyole	Chief John Ntale Nahnumba

The Katukiro (Prime Minister) of Busoga Kingdom is Rt. Hon. Martin Musumba. The office of the Katukiro in the Kingdom is an important and a vital one. The Katukiro is the head of the Kingdom's Government and official spokesperson for the Kyabazinga and the Kingdom.

Busoga Kingdom is administered in the following *(This information is outdated & needs to be updated...)*:

Kamuli District - (4 Counties, 23 Sub Counties & 134 Parishes) - 2 Kings (Bugabula & Bulamogi)
Iganga District - (4 Counties, 25/26 Sub Counties, unknown number of Parishes) - 3 Kings (Kigulu, Luuka & Busiki)   **Mayuge District** - (1 County, 6 Sub-Counties, unknown number of parishes) - 1 King (Bunya)   **Jinja District** - (3 Counties, 11 Sub-Counties, 50 Parishes)

Bugiri District - (1 County, 12 to19) Sub-Counties, unknown Parishes) - Possibly 2 Kings (Bukooli And Banda)

Some attractions and historical sites

Kagulu Hill

Main article: Kagulu Hill

The was the first settlement area for Basoga of Bunyoro origin led by Prince Mukama. Although the cultural value of Kagulu extends to cover a wide area, the remaining and visible landmark is the Kagulu hill. The hill sits in between two roads that divide at the foothill to lead to Gwaya and Iyingo.

The hill, although not yet familiar to many people outside Busoga, Kagulu hill has a breathtaking scenery that gives a clear view of almost the entire Busoga. Kagulu hill is unique in the attractions it offers. It is the only hill in Uganda that has been adapted for tourist climbing, with constructed steps to make it easy for visitors to access the top.

Budhumbula shrine/palace

Main article: Budhumbula shrine/palace

Located 2 km from Kamuli town along the Kamuli-Jinja main road, the site comprises a shrine and the residence of the former Kyabazinga of Busoga, Sir William Wilberforce Kadhumbula Nadiope, who died in 1976. The shrine, covered by beautiful marbles consist of graves of other various members of the royal family, such his father and mother, Yosia Nadiope and Nasikombi respectively.

The other graves found within the shrine are of his son, a former Uganda government Minister, Prince Professor Wilson Nadiope who died in 1991 and his mother Yuliya Babirye Nadiope who died in 2004. The palace's main residence is a legacy of the British colonial government, having been donated by the protectorate government in 1914.

The source of the Nile

Main article: Source of the Nile

The source of the Nile, the second longest river in the world, marked by the discovery of one of the first European explorers, John Speke, is an internationally unique attraction. The tranquility and splendour of both Lake Victoria and River Nile embody great memories of any visitor.

Bujjagali Falls

Main article: Bujagali falls

 This among others, such as the Bujagali ancestral site for the Basoga ancestral spirits at Bujagali falls, includes the numerous rapids along the Nile, virgin nature across the region, and the culture of the people and the great Lake Victoria by no doubt gives Busoga Kingdom its distinct place in tourism.

Lake Victoria

Main article: Lake Victoria

Southern Busoga is lined with the waters of Lake Victoria. The coastline starts from Jinja and goes eastwards, to the border with Kenya.

References

- Fallers, Margaret Chave (1960) *The Eastern Lacustrine Bantu (Ganda and Soga).* Ethnographic survey of Africa: East central Africa, Vol 11. London: International African Institute.
- Cohen, David William (1970). *A survey of interlacustrine chronology. The Journal of African History*, 1970, 11, 2, 177-202.
- Cohen, David William (1986). *Towards a reconstructed past : Historical texts from Busoga, Uganda.* (Fontes historiae africanae). Oxford: Oxford University Press.
- Fallers, Lloyd A (1965) *Bantu Bureaucracy - A Century of Political evolution among the Basoga of Uganda.* Phoenix Books, The University of Chicago.

See also

- Basoga - Basoga ethnic group
- Lusoga - Lusoga Language

External links

- Busoga Kingdom Online [1] A summary of the Busoga Kingdom by the Busoga Kingdom Online - Official website of Busoga
- The Cultural Research Centre - Busoga [2] A resource for literature relating to Basoga

News websites

- New Vision Online - Local East [3] - News, mainly from the Busoga region

Some educational and research institutions

- Busoga University [4] - Home page for Busoga University, formerly Busoga College Mwiri
- Buckley High School [5] - Home page for Buckley High School
- Kiira College Butiki [6] - Home page for Kiira College Butiki
- Busoga College Mwiri [7] - Home page for Busoga College Mwiri
- Busoga College Mwiri [8] - *Not official site*

Bunyoro

Bunyoro-Kitara Kingdom	
Bunyoro Kitara Kingdom	

Motto: FOR GOD AND MY COUNTRY	
Anthem: Unknown **Royal anthem:** Unknown	
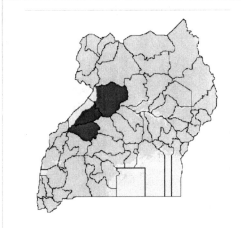 Location of Bunyoro(red) in Uganda(pink)	
Capital (and largest city)	Hoima
Official language(s)	Nyoro
Ethnic groups	Nyoro/Banyoro
Demonym	Bunyoro or Banyoro
Government	Constitutional monarchy
- Omukama	Solomon Iguru I
- Prime Minister	Yabezi Kiiza
Consolidation	16th century

Area		
-	Total	18,578 km^2 3,241 sq mi
-	Water (%)	17
Population		
-	estimate	1,4 million
Currency		Ugandan Shilling (UGX)
Time zone		(UTC+3)
Calling code		256

Bunyoro is a kingdom of western Uganda, and from the sixteenth to the nineteenth century was one of the most powerful kingdoms of East Africa. It is ruled by the Omukama of Bunyoro. The current ruler is Solomon Iguru I, 27th Omukama (king) of Bunyoro-Kitara.

The people of Bunyoro are also known as **Nyoro** or **Banyoro** *(singular: Munyoro)* *(Banyoro means "People of Bunyoro")*; the language spoken is Nyoro *(also known as Runyoro)*. Traditional economies revolved around big-game hunting of elephants, lions, leopards, and crocodiles, but are now agriculturalists who raise bananas, millet, cassava, yams, cotton, tobacco, and coffee.

The people are primarily Christian.

History of the Kingdom

The kingdom of Bunyoro-Kitara was created when the Empire of Kitara broke apart during the 16th century.

At its height, Bunyoro-Kitara controlled almost the entire region between Lake Victoria, Lake Edward, and Lake Albert. One of many small states in the Great Lakes region the earliest stories of the kingdom having great power come from the Rwanda area where there are tales of the Bunyoro raiding the region under a prince named Cwa around 1520. The power of Bunyoro then faded until the mid seventeenth century when a long period of expansion began, with the empire dominating the region by the early eighteenth century.

Bunyoro rose to power by controlling a number of the holiest shrines in the region, the lucrative Kibiro saltworks of Lake Albert, and having the highest quality of metallurgy in the region. This made it the strongest military and economic power in the Great Lakes area.

Bunyoro began to fade in the late eighteenth century due to internal divisions. Buganda seized Kooki and Buddu regions from Bunyoro at the end of the century. In around 1830 the large province of Toro separated, taking with many of the lucrative salt works. To the south Rwanda and Nkore were both growing rapidly, taking over some of the smaller kingdoms that had been Bunyoro's vassals.

Thus by the mid-nineteenth century Bunyoro (also known as **Unyoro** at the time) was a far smaller state, but it was still wealthy controlling lucrative trade routes over Lake Victoria and linking to the coast of the Indian Ocean. Bunyoro especially profited from the trade in ivory. It was, however, continually imperiled by the now potent Buganda (also and still known as Uganda,) which greatly desired taking the trade routes for itself. A long struggle ensued with both arming themselves with European weapons. As a result the capital was moved from Masindi to the less vulnerable Mparo.

In July 1890 agreement the entire region north of Lake Victoria was given to Great Britain. In 1894 Great Britain declared the region its protectorate. King Kabarega of Bunyoro strenuously resisted the efforts of Great Britain, in an alliance with Buganda, to take control of his kingdom. However, in 1899 Kaberega was captured and exiled to the Seychelles and Bunyoro was annexed to the British Empire. Because of their resistance a portion of the Bunyoro kingdom's territory was given to Buganda and Toro.

The country was put under the control of Bugandan administrators. The Bunyoro revolted in 1907; the revolt was put down, and relations improved somewhat. After the region remained loyal to Great Britain in World War I a new agreement was made in 1934 giving the region more autonomy.

Today Bunyoro remains one of the four constituent kingdoms of Uganda.

Bunyoro Kitara Today

During the regime of several dictators such as Idi Amin, the Kingdoms where forcefully disbanded, and where in the time from 1967 to 1994 banned.

In 1993 the Kingdom was re-established and in 1995 the new constitution of Uganda was made, allowing and recognizing, the Kingdoms.

The current Kingdom covers the districts of Hoima district, Masindi district and Kibale district.

The total population of the Kingdom is about between 800.000 and 1.400.000 (depending on sources) living in 250,000-350,000 households. 96% of the population live in rural areas, and only 1% of the population uses electricity for lighting and cooking. More than 92% of the population are poor, and has earnings more than half that of the Ugandan national average, and about 50% of the population is illiterate.

The economic potential in the region is very large, with the Kibiro saltworks, and the possibility of large oil, gas, iron ore and precious stone. Recently the Heritage Gas and Oil Company conducted surveys in the area, indicating the possibility of large crude oil deposits in the area. The area also has large rainforest's with abundance of hardwoods like mahogany, ironwood and others

The Omukama and the other leaders of the area, are working to create a university in the area, that will work primarily with education persons for work with natural resources extraction, hopefully creating prosperity in the area. The university will also work to preserve the high level of cultural heritage in the area.

The King is in general doing a lot of work to improve the living standards of the people. Relations are maintained with the European community via the development organization Association of the Representatives of Bunyoro-Kitara. The King is also working to maintain the traditional bunyoro culture, but in the same time altering the honors of the kingdom in a way that they can be compared to western standards.

Traditions of Bunyoro

For royal traditions see Omukama of Bunyoro.

Relations

The Banyoro was a polygamous people when they could afford it. A lot of marriages did not last and it was quite common to be divorces. Due to this, payment to the girls family wasn't normally given until after several years of marriage.
Premarital sex was also very common.

All families was ruled by the eldest man of the family (Called *Nyineka*), and the village was run by a specially elected elder who was chosen by all the elders in the village and he was known as a *mukuru w'omugongo*.

Birth

A few months after birth the baby would be given a name. This was normally done by a close relative, but the father always had the final saying. Two names are given a personal name, and a traditional *Mpako* name.
The names was often related to specific features on the child, special circumstances around the birth of the child or as a way to honor a former family member. Most of the names are actual words of the Nyoro language

Death

Death was almost always believed to be the work of evil magic, ghosts or similar. Also gossiping was believe to magically affect or harm people.
Death was viewed as being a real being and when a person died to oldest woman of the household would clean the body, cut the hair and beard and close the eyes of the departed. The body was left for viewing and the women and children where allowed to cry/weep, but the men where not. In case the dead was the head of the household as mixture of grain (*called ensigosigo*) where put in his hand, and his children had to take a small part of the grain and eat it - thous passing on his (magical) powers.

After one or two days the body would be wrapped in cloth and a series of rites would be carried out. These are (only for heads of family):

- The nephew must take down the central pole of the hut and throw it in the middle of the compound
- He would also take the bow and eating-bowl of the departed and throw with the pole
- The fireplace in the hut would be extinguished
- A banana plant from the family plantation and a pot of water was also added to the pile
- The family rooster had to be caught and killed
- The main bull of the family's cattle had to be prevented from mating during the mourning (removal of testicles)
- After 4 days of mourning the bull would be killed and eating, thous ending the period of mourning
- The house of the departed would not be used again

The **burial** would not be done in the middle of the day, as it was considered dangerous for the sun to shine directly into the grave. As the body was carried to the grave the women where required to moderate their weeping, and it was forbidden to weep at the grave. Also pregnant women was banned from participating in the funeral as it was believed the negative magical forces related to burial would be to strong for the unborn child to survive.

After the burial the family would cut some of their hair off and put into the grave. After the burial all participants washed themselves very thoroughly, as it was believed that the negative magical forces could harm crops.

If the departed had a grudge or other unfinished business with another family, his mouth and anus would be stuffed with clay, to prevent the ghost from haunting.

A Bunyoro Year

A typical year in Bunyoro is divided into 12 months and it is quite clear what work are to be done these months:

- January (Igesa), there would be harvesting of millet
- February (Nyarakarwa) they did not have much work to do
- March (Ijubyamiyonga) fields were prepared for planting simsim
- May (Rwensisezere) there was not much work
- July (ishanya maro), women would prepare fields for millet
- August (Ikokoba) was the months of burning grass in the millet fields
- September (Isiga) was for planting millet
- November (Rwensenene) was named after grass hoppers
- October (ijuba) was a month of weeding
- December (Nyamiganura or Katuruko) was a month of rejoicing and festivities as there was little work to occupy the people

External links

- Bunyoro-Kitara Kingdom [1]
- NGO that works specific in the Bunyoro-Kitara region of Uganda. Has close connections to the Omukama [2]
- Royal Coat of Arms of Bunyoro-Kitara [3]
- More on the Bunyoro Culture [4]

Buganda

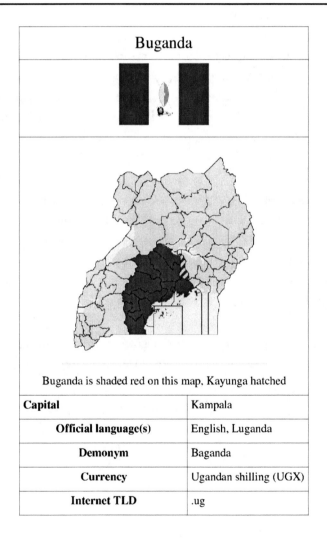

Buganda	
Buganda is shaded red on this map, Kayunga hatched	
Capital	Kampala
Official language(s)	English, Luganda
Demonym	Baganda
Currency	Ugandan shilling (UGX)
Internet TLD	.ug

person	Muganda
people	Baganda
language	Luganda~Oluganda
country	Buganda

Buganda is a subnational kingdom within Uganda. The kingdom of the Ganda people, Buganda is the largest of the traditional kingdoms in present-day Uganda, comprising all of Uganda's Central Region, including the Ugandan capital Kampala, with the exception of the disputed eastern Kayunga District. The 5.5 million *Baganda* (singular *Muganda*; often referred to simply by the root word and adjective, Ganda) make up the largest Ugandan ethnic group, representing approximately 16.9% of Uganda's population.

Buganda has a long and extensive history. Unified in the fourteenth century under the first king Kato Kintu, Buganda became one of the largest and most powerful states in East Africa during the eighteenth and nineteenth centuries. During the Scramble for Africa, and following unsuccessful attempts to retain its independence against British imperialism, Buganda became the centre of the Uganda Protectorate in 1894; the name Uganda, the Swahili term for Buganda, was adopted by British officials. Under British rule, many Baganda acquired status as colonial administrators, and Buganda became a major producer of cotton.

Following Uganda's independence in 1962, the kingdom was abolished by Uganda's dictator Milton Obote in 1966. Following years of dictatorship under Obote and Idi Amin, and following several years of internal divisions among Uganda's ruling National Resistance Movement under Yoweri Museveni, the President of Uganda since 1986, the kingdom was finally restored in 1993. Buganda is now a constitutional monarchy with a large degree of autonomy from the Ugandan state, although tensions between the kingdom and the Ugandan government continue to be a defining feature of Ugandan politics.

Since the restoration of the kingdom in 1993, the king of Buganda, known as the Kabaka, has been Muwenda Mutebi II. He is recognised as the thirty-sixth Kabaka of Buganda. The current queen, known as the Nnabagereka, is Queen Sylvia.

Location

Buganda's boundaries are marked by Lake Victoria to the south, the River Nile to the east, Lake Kyoga to the north and River Kafu to the northwest. To the west, Buganda is bordered by the districts of Isingiro, Kiruhura, Kyenjojo, Kibale, Hoima and Masindi.

The following are the officially recognized counties (amassaza) of Buganda:

1. Ggomba
2. Butambala
3. Kyaddondo
4. Busiro
5. Buddu
6. Bulemeezi
7. Ssingo
8. Kyaggwe
9. Bugerere
10. Buweekula
11. Mawogola
12. Kabula
13. Mawokota
14. Kooki
15. Ssese
16. Buvuma
17. Busujju
18. Buluuli

Secession of Kayunga

In September 2009, some elements alleging to be spokespeople for the Baanyala tribe, declared that Bugerere had seceded from the Kingdom of Buganda. His Majesty, the Kabaka of Buganda, was illegally prohibited by the Yoweri Museveni administration to travel to Bugerere, a decision which unfortunately led to riots and the killing of 30 innocent people – most of whom were Ganda.

Language

The Ganda language (Luganda) is widely spoken in Uganda, and is the most popular second language in Uganda along with English. It is also taught in some primary and secondary schools in Uganda and at Makerere University, Uganda's oldest university and it has an exhaustive dictionary. The Luganda language was also used as a means of instruction in schools outside the region of Buganda prior to Uganda's Independence in 1962.

In literature and common discourse, Buganda is often referred to as Central Uganda. It may be argued that this nomenclature does not refer to Buganda's geographical location, but to its political prominence, and to the fact that Kampala, the nation's capital, is located in Buganda

Geography and environment

Ganda villages, sometimes as large as forty to fifty homes, were generally located on hillsides, leaving hilltops and swampy lowlands uninhabited, to be used for crops or pastures. Early Ganda villages surrounded the home of a chief or headman, which provided a common meeting ground for members of the village. The chief collected tribute from his subjects, provided tribute to the Kabaka, who was the ruler of the kingdom, distributed resources among his subjects, maintained order, and reinforced social solidarity through his decision-making skills. During the late 19th century, Ganda villages became more dispersed as the role of the chiefs diminished in response to political turmoil, population migration, and occasional popular revolts.

History of Buganda

Main article: History of Buganda

The kingdom of Buganda is situated in a swampy hillside that served as a refuge for those escaping rivalries in neighboring Bunyoro. One faction fleeing Bunyoro, under the leadership of Prince Kimera, arrived in Buganda toward the last quarter of the 14th century. The prince molded the already existing refugees in the area into a unified state and became the first Kabaka (ruler) of Buganda.

By the 18th century, the formerly dominant Buyoro kingdom was being eclipsed by Buganda. Consolidating their efforts behind a centralized kingship, the Baganda (people of Buganda) shifted away from defensive strategies and toward expansion. By the mid 19th century, Buganda had doubled and redoubled its territory conquering much on Bunyoro and becoming the dominant state in the region. Newly conquered lands were placed under chiefs nominated by the king. Buganda's armies and the royal tax collectors traveled swiftly to all parts of the kingdom along specially constructed roads which crossed streams and swamps by bridges and viaducts. On Lake Victoria (which the Ganda called Nnalubale), a royal navy of outrigger canoes, commanded by an admiral who was chief of the Lungfish clan, could transport Baganda commandos to raid any shore of the lake. The journalist Henry Morton Stanley visited Buganda in 1875 and provided an estimate of Buganda troop strength. Stanley counted 125,000 troops marching off on a single campaign to the east, where a fleet of 230 war canoes waited to act as auxiliary naval support.

At Buganda's capital, Stanley found a well-ordered town of about 40,000 surrounding the king's palace, which was situated atop a commanding hill. A wall more than four kilometers in circumference surrounded the palace compound, which was filled with grass-roofed houses, meeting halls, and storage buildings. At the entrance to the court burned the royal gombolola (fire), which would only be extinguished when the kabaka died. Thronging the grounds were foreign ambassadors seeking audiences, chiefs going to the royal advisory council, messengers running errands, and a corps of young pages, who served the kabaka while training to become future chiefs. For communication across the kingdom, the messengers were supplemented by drum signals.

The British were impressed with government of Buganda. Under Kabaka Mwanga II, Buganda became a protectorate in 1894. This did not last and the kabarak declared war on Britain in on July 6, 1897. He was defeated at the battle of Buddu on July 20 of the same year. He fled to German East Africa where he was arrested and interned at Bukob. The kabaka later escaped and led a rebel army to retake the kingdom before being defeated once again in 1898 and being exiled to the Seychelles.

The war against Kabaka Mwanga II had been expensive, and the new commissioner of Uganda in 1900, Sir Harry H. Johnston, had orders to establish an efficient administration and to levy taxes as quickly as possible. Sir Johnston approached the chiefs in Buganda with offers of jobs in the colonial administration in return for their collaboration. The chiefs did so but expected their interests (preserving Buganda as a self-governing entity, continuing the royal line of kabakas, and securing private land tenure for themselves and their supporters) to be met. After much hard bargaining, the chiefs ended up with everything they wanted, including one-half of all the land in Buganda. The half left to the British as "Crown Land" was later found to be largely swamp and scrub.

Johnston's Buganda Agreement of 1900 imposed a tax on huts and guns, designated the chiefs as tax collectors, and testified to the continued alliance of British and Baganda interests. The British signed much less generous treaties with the other kingdoms (Toro in 1900, Ankole in 1901, and Bunyoro in 1933) without the provision of large-scale private land tenure.

While in exile, he was received into the Anglican Church, was baptized with the name of Danieri (Daniel). He spent the rest of his life in exile. He died in 1903, aged 35 years. In 1910 his remains were repatriated and buried at Kasubi.[4]

Kabaka Mwanga II Buganda was allowed near complete autonomy and a position as overlord of the other kingdoms.

Demographics

Social structure

Ganda social organization emphasized descent through males. Four or five generations of descendants of one man, related through male forebears, constituted a patrilineage. A group of related lineages constituted a clan. Clan leaders could summon a council of lineage heads, and council decisions affected all lineages within the clan. Many of these decisions regulated marriage, which had always been between two different lineages, forming important social and political alliances for the men of both lineages. Lineage and clan leaders also helped maintain efficient land use practices, and they inspired pride in the group through ceremonies and remembrances of ancestors.

Most lineages maintained links to a home territory (butaka) within a larger clan territory, but lineage members did not necessarily live on butaka land. Men from one lineage often formed the core of a village; their wives, children, and in-laws joined the village. People were free to leave if they became disillusioned with the local leader to take up residence with other relatives or in-laws, and they often did so.

Culture

The family in Buganda is often described as a microcosm of the kingdom. The father is revered and obeyed as head of the family. His decisions are generally unquestioned. A man's social status is determined by those with whom he establishes patron/client relationships, and one of the best means of securing this relationship is through one's children. Baganda children, some as young as three years old, are sent to live in the homes of their social superiors, both to cement ties of loyalty among parents and to provide avenues for social mobility for their children. Even in the 1980s, Baganda children were considered psychologically better prepared for adulthood if they had spent several years living away from their parents at a young age.

A blind Buganda harpist c. 1911

Baganda recognize at a very young age that their superiors, too, live in a world of rules. Social rules require a man to share his wealth by offering hospitality, and this rule applies more stringently to those of higher status. Superiors are also expected to behave with impassivity, dignity, self-discipline, and self-confidence, and adopting these mannerisms sometimes enhances a man's opportunities for success.

Authoritarian control is an important theme of Ganda culture. In precolonial times, obedience to the king was a matter of life and death. However, a second major theme of Ganda culture is the emphasis on individual achievement. An individual's future is not entirely determined by status at birth. Instead, individuals carve out their fortunes by hard work as well as by choosing friends, allies, and patrons carefully.

Ganda culture tolerates social diversity more easily than many other African societies. Even before the arrival of Europeans, many Ganda villages included residents from outside Buganda. Some had arrived in the region as slaves, but by the early 20th century, many non-Baganda migrant workers stayed in Buganda to farm. Marriage with non-Baganda was fairly common, and many Baganda marriages ended in divorce. After independence, Ugandan officials estimated that one-third to one-half of all adults marry more than once during their lives.

Clans of Buganda

As of 2009, there are at least fifty two (52) recognised clans within the kingdom, with at least another four making a claim to clan status. Within this group of clans are four distinct sub-groups which reflect historical waves of immigration to Buganda.

Nansangwa

The oldest clans trace their lineage to the Tonda Kings, who are supposed to have ruled in the region from about 400 AD until about 1300 AD. These six clans are referred to as the Nansangwa, or the indigenous:

1. Lugave (Pangolin)
2. Mmamba (Lungfish)
3. Ngeye (Colobus monkey)
4. Njaza (Reedbuck)
5. Ennyange (White Egret)
6. Fumbe (Civet cat)

Kintu migration

The Abalasangeye dynasty came to power through the conquests of Kabaka Kato Kintu, which are estimated to have occurred sometime between 1200 and 1400 AD.

Thirteen clans are purported to have come with Kintu:

1. Ekkobe (Liana fruit)
2. Mbwa (Dog)
3. Mpeewo (Oribi antelope)
4. Mpologoma (Lion)
5. Namuŋoona (Black crow)
6. Ngo (Leopard)
7. Ŋonge (Otter)
8. Njovu (Elephant)
9. Nkejje (Sprat)
10. Nkima (Brown monkey)
11. Ntalaganya (Blue duiker)
12. Nvubu (Hippopotamus)
13. Nvuma (Pearl)

Kimera migration

Around 1370 AD another wave of immigration assisted by Kabaka Kimera, who was the son of Omulangira Kalemeera. Kabaka Kimera was born in Bunyoro, and returned to Buganda with Jjumba of the Nkima clan and other Buganda elders.

These eleven clans are:

1. Bugeme
2. Butiko (Mushrooms)
3. Kasimba (Genet)
4. Kayozi (Jerboa)
5. Kibe (Fox)
6. Mbogo (Buffalo)
7. Musu/Omusu (Edible rat)
8. Ngabi (Bushbuck)
9. Nkerebwe (Jungle Shrew)
10. Nsuma (Elephant-snout fish)
11. Nseenene (Edible grasshopper)

Other clans

Since Kabaka Kimera twenty further clans have either immigrated to Buganda, or been created internally (largely by kings). These clans are:

1. Abalangira (Descendants of male Royalty from Buganda)
2. Babiito (Descendants of male Royalty from Bunyoro)
3. Basambo
4. Baboobi (Millipede)
5. Kasanke (Finch with black wings and white chest)
6. Kikuba (A pad used to brush aside morning dew when walking through tall grass)
7. Kinyomo (Type of ant)
8. Kiwere (Purple dye plant)
9. Lukato (Stiletto or awl)
10. Mbuzi (Goat)
11. Mpindi (Cowpea)
12. Mutima (Heart)
13. Nakinsige (Brown grass finch)
14. Ndiga (Sheep)
15. Ndiisa (small basket used for coffee berries)
16. Ŋŋaali (Crested Crane)
17. Njobe (Marsh antelope)

18. Nkebuka (Looking back after bush defecation)
19. Nkula (Rhinoceros)
20. Nsunu (Kob)
21. Nte (Ox or cow)
22. Nswaaswa (Monitor lizard)

Economy

The traditional Ganda economy relied on crop cultivation. In contrast with many other East African economic systems, cattle played only a minor role. Many Baganda hired laborers from outside Buganda to herd the Baganda's cattle, for those who owned livestock. Bananas were the most important staple food, providing the economic base for the region's dense population growth. This crop does not require shifting cultivation or bush fallowing to maintain soil fertility, and as a result, Ganda villages were quite permanent. Women did most of the agricultural work, while men often engaged in commerce and politics (and in precolonial times, warfare). Before the introduction of woven cloth, traditional clothing was manufactured from the bark of trees.

See also

- Luganda language
- Kabaka of Buganda
- Mutesa II of Buganda
- Muwenda Mutebi II of Buganda
- Baganda Music
- The legend of Kintu
- Uganda Cowries
- Kanzu
- Gomesi
- King's African Rifles KAR

References

pnb:بوگانڈا

Rwenzururu region

Kingdom of Rwenzururu Obusinga Bwa Rwenzururu	
Kingdom	
 ← **Life span?**	
 Flag	
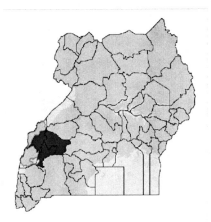 Location of the Kingdom of Rwenzururu in Uganda in green, and the current borders of the Kingdom of Toro in red	
Capital	Kasese
Language(s)	English, Konzo
Government	Monarchy
King of Rwenzururu	
- 1963-1966	Isaya Mukirania
- 1966-1982, 2009-	Charles Mumbere
Historical era	Cold War
- Established	February 13, 1963

- Disestablished	*Enter end year*

Rwenzururu is a region in the Rwenzori Mountains of Uganda on the border of the Democratic Republic of the Congo, as well as an armed historical movement to achieve either autonomy or sovereignty for that region, and the name of a kingdom declared in that region. It includes the Bundibugyo and Kasese districts.

Background

Road in Rwenzori region valley

The Rwenzururu region is inhabited by the Konjo and Amba peoples. In the early 1900s, these two tribes were integrated into the Kingdom of Toro as a political maneuver by the British colonialists: the neighboring Bunyoro monarchy was anti-colonialist (see 1907 Nyangire rebellion) and the British wished to strengthen the pro-British Toro. The Bakonjo and Baamba initially accepted being arbitrarily made subjects of the Toro monarch with resignation, but asked the Uganda Protectorate to provide them their own district in the 1950s, separate from Toro District. The movement declared that they were not part of the Toro Kingdom on 30 June 1962, three months before national independence.

Conflict and kingdom

After their request was denied by the colonial authorities, the Bakonjo and Baamba launched a low-intensity guerrilla war that continued through independence. The movement carrying out the armed struggle was named "Rwenzururu." While the movement began to achieve recognition as a separate district, it eventually became a movement to secede and form their own kingdom. The movement declared an independent **Kingdom of Rwenzururu** on 30 June 1963, three months before national independence, with Isaya Mukirania as king. The violence reached a height in 1963 and 1964, when Toro soldiers massacred many Konjo and Amba people as they sought to control the lower valleys. The Ugandan army intervened against the separatists, doing such significant damage to the Rwenzururu that the movement was suppressed for some time. However, the movement achieved fame through a local folk epic.

The Rwenzururu gradually re-established itself in the collapse of the regime of Idi Amin in 1979. As government soldiers retreated in the Uganda-Tanzania War, the Rwenzururu looted the weapons and supplies left behind. Thus well-armed, the Rwenzururu was once again able to pose a serious threat to regional control from 1979 to 1982. However, in 1982, the administration of President Milton Obote negotiated a settlement with the Rwenzururu leaders in which they agreed to abandon the goal of secession in exchange for "a degree of local autonomy," the appointment of Bakonjo and Baamba to government administrative posts and economic benefits such as vehicles and educational scholarships to be distributed by local elders. During the negotiations, the government preferred direct talks, as they believed third-party mediation would give legitimacy to the Rwenzururu claim.

Amon Bazira, had been a key person in the negotiations between the Rwenzururu and Obote government. His insight was that the Rwenzururu was a largely middle class organization that could be placated with commercial prizes. He later approached President Mobutu Sese Seko of Zaire and President Daniel arap Moi of Kenya, who both had grounds for disliking the new Ugandan government led by Yoweri Museveni, for support for new Bakonjo rebellion under an organization called the **National Army for the Liberation of Uganda** (NALU). Bazira was shot dead in the State House in Nakuru, Kenya in 1993, a probable target of Ugandan agents. In 1995, Sudanese agents engineered the merging of the remnants of NALU with the Uganda Muslim Liberation Army (UMLA) and the Baganda monarchist Allied Democratic Movement (ADM) in order to give these latter organizations a local constituency, creating the Allied Democratic Forces.

Government recognition

A survey carried out by Makerere University found that 87% of the local population in Rwenzururu favored the creation of a kingdom. In 2005, President Yoweri Museveni directed a ministerial committee headed by Second Deputy Prime Minister and Minister for Public Service Henry Kajura to investigate the Rwenzururu claim to a kingdom and issue a report of his findings. The report stated that over 80% of the Bakonjo and Baamba favored the creation of a kingdom with Charles Mumbere as the *Omusinga* (King). It further found that there is no historical claim for a Rwenzururu kingdom or a group of people called **Banyarwenzururu**, but recommended that the government bow to the wishes of the people. Pursuant to the recommendations of the Kajura report, on 17 March 2008 the Ugandan Cabinet endorsed the Kingdom of Rwenzururu as a cultural institution. Three contenders for the throne criticized the government's recognition of Mumbere as *Omusinga*.

References

- Forrest, Joshua (2004). *Subnationalism in Africa: ethnicity, alliances, and politics* [1]. Lynne Rienner Publishers. ISBN 9781588262271. Retrieved 6 June 2009.
- Prunier, Gérard (2009). *Africa's World War: Congo, the Rwandan Genocide, and the Making of a Continental Catastrophe*. Oxford: Oxford University Press. ISBN 978-0-19-537420-9.
- Rothchild, Donald S. (1997). *Managing ethnic conflict in Africa: pressures and incentives for cooperation* [2]. Brookings Institution Press. ISBN 9780815775935. Retrieved 6 June 2009.

Further reading

- Arthur Syahuku-Muhindo, "The Rwenzururu Movement and the Democratic Struggle," in M. Mamdani and J. Oloka-Onyango, eds., *Uganda: Studies in Living Conditions, Popular Movements and Constitutionalism* (Vienna: JEP Books, 1994), 273-317.

External links

- Official Site [2]
- "Uganda: Rwenzururu Wants Recognition - Mumbere" [3], *New Vision*, 26 September 2007 (accessed 6 June 2009)

Culture and Arts

Culture of Uganda

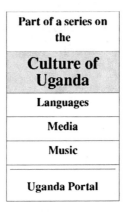

Part of a series on the
Culture of Uganda
Languages
Media
Music
Uganda Portal

The **culture of Uganda** is made up of a diverse range of ethnic groups. Lake Kyoga forms the northern boundary for the Bantu-speaking peoples, who dominate much of east, central and southern Africa. In Uganda they include the Baganda and several other tribes. In the north live the Lango and the Acholi, who speak Nilotic languages. To the east are the Iteso and Karamojong, who speak a Nilotic language. A few Pygmies live isolated in the rainforests of western Uganda.

Music

Main article: music of Uganda

Each ethnic group has its musical history; songs are passed down from generation to generation. *Ndigindi* and *entongoli*(lyres), *ennanga* (harp), *amadinda* (xylophone, see Baganda Music) and *lukeme* (lamellophone ("thumb piano")) are commonly played instruments. An Acholi, Okot p'Bitek, is one of Uganda's most famous writers of folklore, satirical poems and songs. His book *Song of Lawino (1966)* describes the stories told in Acholi songs.

Religion

Christians make up 85.1% of Uganda's population.[ciafactbook] There were sizeable numbers of Sikhs and Hindus in the country until Asians were expelled in 1972 by Idi Amin, following an alleged dream, although many are now returning following an invitation from the new president, Yoweri Museveni. There are also Muslims.

Sport

The Uganda national football team, nicknamed *The Cranes*, is the national team of Uganda and is controlled by the Federation of Uganda Football Associations. They have never qualified for the World Cup finals; their best finish in the African Nations Cup was second in 1978. Cricket is also one of major sports having made the World Cup in 1975 as part of the East African cricket team. Furthermore Uganda also

Young boys playing a casual game of football (soccer) in Arua District

engages in basketball however this is not well developed, there is a national league played by college students and a few high school students. Uganda hosted and won a regional tournament in 2006 other countries that participated were Kenya, Tanzania, Rwanda and Burundi. Growing in populariy in the country is rugby, the National team has been growing stronger as evidenced by more frequent victories and close games against African powerhouses like Namibia and Morocco.

Cuisine

Main article: Cuisine of Uganda

The Cuisine of Uganda consists of traditional cooking with English, Arab and Asian (especially Indian) influences. Like the cuisines of most countries, it varies in complexity, from the most basic, a starchy filler with a sauce of beans or meat, to several-course meals served in upper-class homes and high-end restaurants.

Main dishes are usually centred on a sauce or stew of groundnuts, beans or meat. The starch traditionally comes from ugali (maize meal) or matoke (boiled and mashed green banana), in the South, or an ugali made from pearl millet in the North. Cassava, yam and African sweet potato are also eaten; the more affluent include white (often called "Irish") potato and rice in their diets. Soybean was promoted as a healthy food staple in the 1970s and this is also used, especially for breakfast. Chapati, an Asian flatbread, is also part of Ugandan cuisine.

Chicken, fish (usually fresh, but there is also a dried variety, reconstituted for stewing), beef, goat and mutton are all commonly eaten, although among the rural poor there would have to be a good reason for slaughtering a large animal such as a goat or a cow and *nyama*, (Swahili word for "meat") would not be eaten every day.

Various leafy greens are grown in Uganda. These may be boiled in the stews, or served as side dishes in fancier homes. Amaranth (*dodo*), nakati, and *borr* are examples of regional greens.

Ugali which is maize flour is mixed with water to make porridge for breakfast mainly for children. For main means, maize flour is added to some water in a saucepan and stirred into the ugali is firm like American cornbread. It is then turned out onto a serving plate and cut into individual slices (or served onto individual plates in the kitchen).

Language

Main article: Languages of Uganda

Uganda is ethnologically diverse, with at least forty languages in usage. Luganda is the most common language. English is the official language of Uganda, even though only a relatively small proportion of the population speaks it. Access to economic and political power is almost impossible without having mastered that language. The East African lingua franca Swahili is relatively widespread as a trade language and was made an official national language of Uganda in September 2005.[swahili] Luganda, a language widespread in central Uganda, has been the official vernacular language in education for central Uganda for a long time.[luganda]

Clothing

In Uganda, the Kanzu is the national dress of men in the country. Women from central and eastern Uganda wear a dress with a sash tied around the waist and large exaggerated shoulders called a Gomesi. Women from the west, northwestern drape a long cloth round their waists and shoulders called (Suuka). Women from the southwest wear a long baggy skirt and tie a short matching cloth across their shoulders.

See also

- Uganda National Cultural Centre
- Seguku Women's Association (SeWA)

Notes and references

Notes

1. CIA Factbook Profile on Uganda [2]
2. IPP (Tanzania) [1],Britannica [2]
3. Mukama 1991

References

- Mukama, Ruth G. (1991) 'Recent developments in the language situation and prospects for the future', pp. 334-350 in *Changing Uganda*, eds. Holger Bernt Hansen & Michael Twaddle, Fountain Publishers, 1991, ISBN
- Trowell, Margaret; Wachsmann, Klaus (1953) Tribal Crafts of Uganda, Oxford, 1953

Ugandan cuisine

Ugandan cuisine consists of traditional cooking with English, Arab and Asian (especially Indian) influences. Like the cuisines of most countries, it varies in complexity, from the most basic, a starchy filler with a sauce of beans or meat, to several-course meals served in upper-class homes and high-end restaurants. [*citation needed*]

Main dishes are usually centered on a sauce or stew of groundnuts, beans or meat. The starch traditionally comes from ugali (maize meal) or matoke (boiled and mashed green banana), in the South, or an ugali made from millet in the North. Cassava, yam and African sweet potato are also eaten; the more affluent include white (often called "Irish") potato and rice in their diets. Soybean was promoted as a healthy food staple in the 1970s and this is also used, especially for breakfast. Chapati, an Asian flatbread, is also part of Ugandan cuisine.

Chicken, fish (usually fresh, but there is also a dried variety, reconstituted for stewing), beef, goat and mutton are all commonly eaten, although among the rural poor there would have to be a good reason for slaughtering a large animal such as a goat or a cow and *nyama*, (Swahili word for "meat") would not be eaten every day.

Various leafy greens are grown in Uganda. These may be boiled in the stews, or served as side dishes in fancier homes. Amaranth (*dodo*), nakati, and *borr* are examples of regional greens.

Ugali is cooked up into a thick porridge for breakfast. For main meals, white flour is added to the saucepan and stirred into the ugali until the consistency is firm. It is then turned out onto a serving plate and cut into individual slices (or served onto individual plates in the kitchen).

Fruits are plentiful and regularly eaten, as in the Western World, as snacks or dessert. Europeans introduced cake and this is also popular.

Some traditional food names

- Ugali - usually from maize but also other starches, regional names include *posho* and *kwon*. Ugandan expatriates make ugali from cornmeal, masa harina or grits.
- Groundnut - peanuts are a vital staple and groundnut sauce is probably the most commonly eaten one.
- Sim-sim - sesame - used particularly in the north, roasted sesame paste is mixed into a stew of beans or greens and served as a side dish, sesame paste may be served as a condiment; a candy is made from roasted sesame seeds with sugar or honey.
- Matoke - Mashed plantain that used as opposed to mashed potato. Usually used in a main course.

Snacks

- roasted groundnuts served in a spill of paper
- *samusa* (samousa, samosa) -- Indian samosas have been completely assimilated into the local cuisine, as have chapati and curry
- *mugati naamaggi* (bread and eggs). Originally an Arab dish, it's wheat dough spread into a thin pancake, filled with minced meat and raw egg, and then folded into a neat parcel and fried on a hotplate.
- *nsenene* is an unusual food item: a seasonal delicacy of a type of grasshopper
- *nswaa* served similarly to nsenene but made of white ant

Beverages

Both traditional and western beers are probably the most widely available alcoholic beverage across Uganda. Pombe is the generic word for locally made fermented beer, usually from banana or millet. Tonto is a traditional fermented drink made from bananas. Waragi is the generic term for distilled spirits and these also vary, see for example Uganda Waragi a brand name for clear or yellow gin.

Tea (*chai*) and coffee (*kawa*) are popular beverages and important cash crops. These can be served English-style or spiced (*chai masala*).

Coca-cola, Pepsi and Fanta all made inroads in the Ugandan market and soda became very popular.

External links

- Ugandan cuisine: Food for the soul [1], *Daily Monitor*, October 9, 2008

Music of Uganda

Part of a series on the
Culture of Uganda
Languages
Media
Music
Uganda Portal

The African country of Uganda has had a turbulent history in the 20th century, and music has been an integral part of the nation's development.

The first form of music genre in Uganda was kadongo kamu (single guitar).

In the 80's Jimmy Katumba and his band The Ebonies were popular. In the late 1980s and 1990s the album *Born in Africa* by Philly Lutaaya, in exile in Sweden, was a hit. The songs on this album remain very popular in Uganda, the musicians remain among the best-known Ugandan musicians.

In the 1990s a Swedish producer produced a similar album in Uganda by a supergroup of Ugandan musicians called Big Five. Also during the 90s, Geoffrey Oryema recorded several critically acclaimed albums on Peter Gabriel's Real World Studios|Real World label. Lately new artists have produced music that blends western styles with East African rhythms. Recently, the Shropshire Music Foundation has been working with Ugandan children in war-torn communities to use music as a unifying factor.

Kampala is the center for Ugandan music, especially in the area of Wandegeya, which is the home of kadongo kamu. The most renowned musician of this style was Bernard Kabanda. There have been many contributors of Kadongo Kamu, which means one guitar as the leading instrument used to be one guitar over the years. Kadongo Kamu never used to appeal to the young kids in the towns especially the learned ones as much as it did to the older people however it was always educational and informative.

A new style of music has developed in East Africa in recent years called utake which comes from the first letters of Tanzania. Utake includes elements of music of Tanzania|Tanzanian, music of Kenya and Ugandan music.

Gospel music is gaining in popularity in Uganda, and among the artists that have contributed to this success are Ivan Woods [pamoja president], Martin Seku, Judith Babirye, Wilson Bugembe, Betty Namaganda, Betty Nakibuka, Afandae Lanneck, The kingdom Dancers and others. Roots reggae, ragga, dancehall and reggaeton music are also popular in Uganda.

Top artists

Top artists in Uganda include Jose Chameleon (heavy weight), Bebe Cool locally called Munene Munene, Bobi Wine who is called ghetto president, Radio and Weasel (also operating as Goodlyfe Crew), another sammie e with an exceptional talent, Ragga Dee and Madoxx Ssematimba, Babaluku and The Bataka Squad founders of Luga Flow which promotes rapping in your mother tongue. These artists are also doing well on the international scene.

Buganda

Main article: Baganda music

Buganda is the Central region of Uganda. The people in this region are known as the Baganda (one of the largest tribes in Uganda). This region has also had one of the longest reigning monarchies in Uganda. The Kingdom of Buganda is ruled by a king (known as "Kabaka"), who traditionally has been the main patron of the music of Buganda. Music includes massive and sacred drums, and a variety of vibrant dances such as Bakisimba, Nankasa, Amaggunju [an exclusive dance developed in the palace for the Kabaka]. The Baganda also have a wide variety of melodic musical instruments ranging from Chordophones like the ennanga harp and the entongoli lyre, lamellophones, aerophones, drums and idiophones; this region boasts one of the largest xylophone (called "*Madinda*") traditions in Sub Saharan Africa. There are two types of xylophones, the amadinda and the larger akadinda. Famous musicians from this region include Albert Ssempeke, Evalisto Muyinda, Nandujja, the late Peterson T. Mutebi and the late Elly Wamala, among others.

Basoga

Music of Busoga has similarities to the music of Buganda. The Busoga xylophone, called *embaire*, is used in the courtly music of the Busoga court. The compository principles of embaire music are similar to those of the *amadinda* music of Buganda.

Lango

The Langi live in the central area of Uganda, north of Lake Kyoga. The *okeme* (thumb piano) is popular since having been brought in the early 20th century by Congolese porters. Group vocals akin to rapping are common, and can including rhythmic dancing featuring stomping and jumping.

References

- Sandahl, Sten. "Exiles and Traditions". 2000. In Broughton, Simon and Ellingham, Mark with McConnachie, James and Duane, Orla (Ed.), *World Music, Vol. 1: Africa, Europe and the Middle East*, pp 698–701. Rough Guides Ltd, Penguin Books. ISBN 1-85828-636-0
- Kubik, Gerhard "Xylophonspiel im Süden von Uganda" (1988). In: Kubik, Gerhard Zum Verstehen Afrikanischer Musik, Aufsätze, Reihe: Ethnologie: Forschung und Wissenschaft, Bd. 7, 2., aktualisierte und ergänzte Auflage, 2004, 448 S., ISBN 3-8258-7800-7 [1] (in German language).

External links

- Ekimeeza [2]
- Infinit3 Records studios [3] Music from Uganda and East Africa
- Kingdom Dancers [4]
- Uganda music lyrics, audio, video, info [5]
- Uganda Videos - Watch and download Ugandan music videos [6]
- Ugandan Music Information [7]
- Interviews with Ugandan musicians at UGPulse.com [8]
- Traditional music, artists and instruments from Uganda [9]
- 256UP for the latest on Ugandan HipHop, RnB [10]
- Uganda Music Videos on Hipipo.com [11]
- Uganda Music News, Gossip, Celebrities and Music Videos [12]

Transportation

Boda-boda

Boda-boda (or bodaboda) is a bicycle taxi, originally in East Africa (from English *border-border*). The bicycle rider can also be called boda-boda.

Origin

The boda-boda taxis are part of the African bicycle culture; they started in the 1960s and 1970s and are still spreading from their origin on the Kenyan - Ugandan border to other regions. The name originated from a need to transport people across the "no-mans-land" between the border posts without the paperwork involved with using motor vehicles crossing

on the way to the village

the international border. This started in southern border crossing town of Busia (Uganda), where there is over half a mile between the gates, and quickly spread to the northern border town of Malaba (Kenya). The bicycle owners would shout out *boda-boda* (border-to-border) to potential customers - not to be confused with *poda-poda*, which is a form of shared taxi in Sierra Leone.

Bicycles in use and type of work

Indian or Chinese standard roadster bicycles are used with locally made carriers and a cushion to transport passengers and goods. There are big advantages compared to the expensive, slow and heavy Cycle rickshaw used in Asia.

In many East African and Central African cities and villages, professional bodaboda taxi-drivers are common. Bodaboda organizations have been founded in many towns. They help to minimize the risks (dangerous driving, badly maintained bikes) by registering and licensing their members.

Motorbikes replacing bicycles

While the boda-boda bicycle is still spreading to other areas, in its area of origin, especially in cities in Kenya and Uganda, the bicycles are more and more replaced by motorbikes. The motorbike-taxis have taken the name bodaboda as well, though in much of Uganda, the Swahili term for motorbike, **piki-piki,** is used to describe motorbike boda-bodas. In 2004 it was estimated that more than 200 000 men in Uganda were working as bicycle bodaboda and already almost 90 000 as motorized motorbike bodaboda.

Moped boda-boda in Uganda

Okada or **Achaba** is the Nigerian equivalent to motorbike bodaboda.

See also

- Auto rickshaw
- Cycle rickshaw
- Motorcycle taxi
- Rickshaw
- Taxicab
- Tricycle
- Utility cycling

External links

- BodaBoda for the Whole of Africa [1]
- [2] (German)
- Africa Bicycle & Sustainable Transport Advocacy Organizations & Clubs [3]
- [4]

Entebbe International Airport

Entebbe International Airport	
IATA: EBB – ICAO: HUEN	
Summary	
Airport type	Civilian and Military
Operator	Civil Aviation Authority of Uganda
Serves	Entebbe, Kampala, Mukono
Location	Entebbe, Uganda
Hub for	{{{hub}}}
Elevation AMSL	3,782 ft / 1,153 m
Coordinates	00°02′40″N 32°26′33″E

Runways			
Direction	**Length**		**Surface**
	m	**ft**	
17/35	3,658	12,000	Asphalt
12/30	2,408	7,900	Asphalt
Source: DAFIF			

Entebbe International Airport (IATA: **EBB**, ICAO: **HUEN**) is the principal international airport of Uganda. It is located near the town of Entebbe, on the shores of Lake Victoria, and about 35 km (21 miles) from the capital, Kampala. The main offices of the Civil Aviation Authority of Uganda are located at the airport.

The airport was first constructed in 1928/1929: the first aircraft to use the new airfield were RAF Fairey IIIs of the Cairo-Cape flight which landed on the 900 yards (820 m) grass runway on 17 February 1929. In January 1932 Imperial Airways began to use Entebbe on their Cape-to-Cairo mail services: at this stage, radio was installed. By 1935, the grass runway surfaces had been replaced by murram. In 1944-45 the main runway (12/30) was asphalted and extended to 1600 yards (1500 m).

On 10 November 1951 the airport was formally re-opened after the facilities had been extended further: runway 12/30 was now 3300 yards (3000 m), in preparation for services by the de Havilland Comet. Finally, the existing control tower of the "old airport" was constructed in 1957/58.

The current passenger terminal building was constructed in the mid to late 1970s, together with runway 17/35: the old runway 12/30 was shortened to its current length. The Old Entebbe airport is now used by Uganda's military forces and was the scene of a hostage rescue operation by Israeli Sayeret Matkal, dubbed Operation Entebbe, in 1976, after an Arab-German hijacking of Air France Flight 139 out of Tel Aviv.

The scene of that particular rescue was "the old airport", which was recently demolished except for its control tower. In late 2007, a domestic terminal was constructed at the site of the old airport, leaving the "new airport" to handle International flights exclusively. Entebbe International Airport served 720,000 International passengers in 2007. (+10.7% vs. 2006). The unofficial figure of arrivals in 2008 is estimated at 850,000 (+18.1% vs. 2006)

Entebbe Airport is a Cooperative Security Location of the United States military. Entebbe airport uses the jetway boarding bridge system.

Airlines and destinations

Scheduled passenger airlines

Airlines	Destinations
Air Burundi	Bujumbura
Air Uganda	Dar es Salaam, Juba, Kigali, Nairobi, Mombasa, Zanzibar
British Airways	London-Heathrow
Brussels Airlines	Brussels, Kigali, Nairobi
Eagle Air	Arua, Gulu, Moyo, Kidepo, Kitgum, Pakuba, Juba, Yei, Bunia
EgyptAir	Cairo
Emirates	Dubai, Addis Ababa
Ethiopian Airlines	Addis Ababa, Kigali
Feeder Airlines	Juba
Fly540	Nairobi
Kenya Airways	Nairobi

KLM	Amsterdam
Precision Air	Kilimanjaro, Mwanza
Royal Daisy Airlines	Juba
RwandAir	Kigali
South African Airways	Johannesburg
Turkish Airlines	Istanbul-Atatürk
United Airlines Limited	Gulu, Arua,Khiswala-AYZ

Cargo airlines

Airlines	Destinations
Avient Aviation	Liège
Martinair	Amsterdam
Uganda Air Cargo	Dubai, Johannesburg, Frankfurt, London

Sunset over Entebbe

Passenger terminal building

Old Entebbe International Airport

Entebbe old tower in 2008.

A Fly540 ATR 42 at Entebbe

A Lockheed L-100-20 Hercules in UN livery at Entebbe, preparing for yet another trip to Eastern Congo

Air Uganda McDonnell Douglas MD-80 taxiing to runway 17

Entebbe old tower

See also

- Civil Aviation Authority of Uganda
- List of airports in Uganda

Sources

- http://travelvideo.tv/news/more.php?id=15752_0_1_0_M
- http://www.caa.co.ug/

External links

- Uganda Civil Aviation Authority [1]
- Current weather for HUEN [2] at NOAA/NWS
- Accident history for EBB [3] at Aviation Safety Network

Article Sources and Contributors

Uganda *Source*: http://en.wikipedia.org/?oldid=390262520 *Contributors*: DisillusionedBitterAndKnackered

History of Uganda *Source*: http://en.wikipedia.org/?oldid=385070012 *Contributors*: LilHelpa

Geography of Uganda *Source*: http://en.wikipedia.org/?oldid=385308867 *Contributors*:

English language *Source*: http://en.wikipedia.org/?oldid=390472189 *Contributors*: VictorianMutant

Luganda *Source*: http://en.wikipedia.org/?oldid=390069462 *Contributors*:

Kampala *Source*: http://en.wikipedia.org/?oldid=386113294 *Contributors*: Peaceworld111

Makindye Division *Source*: http://en.wikipedia.org/?oldid=363868152 *Contributors*:

Nakasero *Source*: http://en.wikipedia.org/?oldid=368261338 *Contributors*: Xenocidic

Kawempe Division *Source*: http://en.wikipedia.org/?oldid=363867796 *Contributors*:

Kasubi hill *Source*: http://en.wikipedia.org/?oldid=368092266 *Contributors*: Xenocidic

Nakawa Division *Source*: http://en.wikipedia.org/?oldid=363868540 *Contributors*:

Lubaga Division *Source*: http://en.wikipedia.org/?oldid=363868064 *Contributors*:

Kasubi Tombs *Source*: http://en.wikipedia.org/?oldid=387435123 *Contributors*:

Mengo, Uganda *Source*: http://en.wikipedia.org/?oldid=368130027 *Contributors*:

Kibuli *Source*: http://en.wikipedia.org/?oldid=368062201 *Contributors*:

Namirembe hill *Source*: http://en.wikipedia.org/?oldid=368261450 *Contributors*: Xenocidic

Lubaga *Source*: http://en.wikipedia.org/?oldid=385819574 *Contributors*: Hmains

Kampala Hill *Source*: http://en.wikipedia.org/?oldid=387492570 *Contributors*:

Kampala Sheraton Hotel *Source*: http://en.wikipedia.org/?oldid=383730756 *Contributors*: Jamesluckard

Makindye *Source*: http://en.wikipedia.org/?oldid=367547278 *Contributors*: Xenocidic

Kololo *Source*: http://en.wikipedia.org/?oldid=381644463 *Contributors*: Shakibkimz

Uganda Museum *Source*: http://en.wikipedia.org/?oldid=350843758 *Contributors*: Americanfreedom

Uganda National Cultural Centre *Source*: http://en.wikipedia.org/?oldid=381472967 *Contributors*: Kratvej4

Nakasero Market *Source*: http://en.wikipedia.org/?oldid=328192737 *Contributors*: Starzynka

Port Bell *Source*: http://en.wikipedia.org/?oldid=383987680 *Contributors*: 1 anonymous edits

Lubiri *Source*: http://en.wikipedia.org/?oldid=367523108 *Contributors*: Bender235

Lake Albert (Africa) *Source*: http://en.wikipedia.org/?oldid=386916499 *Contributors*: Jauhienij

Entebbe *Source*: http://en.wikipedia.org/?oldid=381803671 *Contributors*: G. Capo

Rwenzori Mountains *Source*: http://en.wikipedia.org/?oldid=387386776 *Contributors*:

Toro Kingdom *Source*: http://en.wikipedia.org/?oldid=375477000 *Contributors*: AjaxSmack

Ankole *Source*: http://en.wikipedia.org/?oldid=375477186 *Contributors*: AjaxSmack

Busoga *Source*: http://en.wikipedia.org/?oldid=383320466 *Contributors*: 1 anonymous edits

Bunyoro *Source*: http://en.wikipedia.org/?oldid=390490846 *Contributors*: FT2

Buganda *Source*: http://en.wikipedia.org/?oldid=380372891 *Contributors*: Kwamikagami

Rwenzururu region *Source*: http://en.wikipedia.org/?oldid=366270487 *Contributors*: Kwamikagami

Culture of Uganda *Source*: http://en.wikipedia.org/?oldid=367439347 *Contributors*: Jusdafax

Ugandan cuisine *Source*: http://en.wikipedia.org/?oldid=363263253 *Contributors*: 1 anonymous edits

Music of Uganda *Source*: http://en.wikipedia.org/?oldid=370469393 *Contributors*: 1 anonymous edits

Boda-boda *Source*: http://en.wikipedia.org/?oldid=366653084 *Contributors*: DisillusionedBitterAndKnackered

Entebbe International Airport *Source*: http://en.wikipedia.org/?oldid=386968114 *Contributors*: 1 anonymous edits

Image Sources, Licenses and Contributors

File:Flag of Uganda.svg *Source*: http://bibliocm.bibliolabs.com/mwAnon/index.php?title=File:Flag_of_Uganda.svg *License*: Public Domain *Contributors*: User:Nightstallion

File:LocationUganda.svg *Source*: http://bibliocm.bibliolabs.com/mwAnon/index.php?title=File:LocationUganda.svg *License*: Creative Commons Attribution-Sharealike 2.5 *Contributors*: User:Vardion

Image:Yoweri Museveni.jpg *Source*: http://bibliocm.bibliolabs.com/mwAnon/index.php?title=File:Yoweri_Museveni.jpg *License*: Public Domain *Contributors*: White House photo by Paul Morse

Image:Ug-map.png *Source*: http://bibliocm.bibliolabs.com/mwAnon/index.php?title=File:Ug-map.png *License*: Public Domain *Contributors*: Central Intelligence Agency

Image:Uganda Districts.png *Source*: http://bibliocm.bibliolabs.com/mwAnon/index.php?title=File:Uganda_Districts.png *License*: Public Domain *Contributors*: User:Rarelibra

Image:Uganda-Development.JPG *Source*: http://bibliocm.bibliolabs.com/mwAnon/index.php?title=File:Uganda-Development.JPG *License*: Creative Commons Attribution-Sharealike 3.0 *Contributors*: Andrew Regan

Image:Languages of Uganda.png *Source*: http://bibliocm.bibliolabs.com/mwAnon/index.php?title=File:Languages_of_Uganda.png *License*: unknown *Contributors*: AnonMoos, Davius, Electionworld, Mahahahaneapneap, Mark Dingemanse

Image:Uganda - Ruwenzori Mountain Lady.jpg *Source*: http://bibliocm.bibliolabs.com/mwAnon/index.php?title=File:Uganda_-_Ruwenzori_Mountain_Lady.jpg *License*: Creative Commons Attribution 2.0 *Contributors*: Dylan Walters

Image:Football in full swing (501839950).jpg *Source*: http://bibliocm.bibliolabs.com/mwAnon/index.php?title=File:Football_in_full_swing_(501839950).jpg *License*: Creative Commons Attribution 2.0 *Contributors*: Sanjoy Ghosh from Austin, Texas, USA

File:Ugandaoflag.gif *Source*: http://bibliocm.bibliolabs.com/mwAnon/index.php?title=File:Ugandaoflag.gif *License*: GNU Free Documentation License *Contributors*: Blowback, Fry1989, Himasaram, Liftarn, Mnmazur, Szoltys

Image:Acholiland, Uganda.png *Source*: http://bibliocm.bibliolabs.com/mwAnon/index.php?title=File:Acholiland,_Uganda.png *License*: unknown *Contributors*: Ji-Elle, Liftarn, Mahahahaneapneap, Mark Dingemanse, Yuval Madar

Image:PD-icon.svg *Source*: http://bibliocm.bibliolabs.com/mwAnon/index.php?title=File:PD-icon.svg *License*: Public Domain *Contributors*: User:Duesentrieb, User:Rfl

Image:Uganda_sat.png *Source*: http://bibliocm.bibliolabs.com/mwAnon/index.php?title=File:Uganda_sat.png *License*: unknown *Contributors*: Cwolfsheep, Ezeu, Lokal Profil, Martin H.

Image:Uganda Topography.png *Source*: http://bibliocm.bibliolabs.com/mwAnon/index.php?title=File:Uganda_Topography.png *License*: Public Domain *Contributors*: User:Sadalmelik

File:Anglospeak.svg *Source*: http://bibliocm.bibliolabs.com/mwAnon/index.php?title=File:Anglospeak.svg *License*: Public Domain *Contributors*: User:Shardz

File:English dialects1997 modified.svg *Source*: http://bibliocm.bibliolabs.com/mwAnon/index.php?title=File:English_dialects1997_modified.svg *License*: Public Domain *Contributors*: User:Jak, user:Mwtoews

File:Origins of English PieChart 2D.svg *Source*: http://bibliocm.bibliolabs.com/mwAnon/index.php?title=File:Origins_of_English_PieChart_2D.svg *License*: Public Domain *Contributors*: User:Jak

File:KampalaSkyline.jpg *Source*: http://bibliocm.bibliolabs.com/mwAnon/index.php?title=File:KampalaSkyline.jpg *License*: GNU Free Documentation License *Contributors*: User:Omoo

File:Uganda location map.svg *Source*: http://bibliocm.bibliolabs.com/mwAnon/index.php?title=File:Uganda_location_map.svg *License*: Creative Commons Attribution-Sharealike 3.0 *Contributors*: NordNordWest

File:Red pog.svg *Source*: http://bibliocm.bibliolabs.com/mwAnon/index.php?title=File:Red_pog.svg *License*: Public Domain *Contributors*: User:Andux

Image:Kampala Road 1950s.jpg *Source*: http://bibliocm.bibliolabs.com/mwAnon/index.php?title=File:Kampala_Road_1950s.jpg *License*: Public Domain *Contributors*: unknown, but since this is a postcard image, it was created and published in Uganda

Image:Burton Street, Kampala.jpg *Source*: http://bibliocm.bibliolabs.com/mwAnon/index.php?title=File:Burton_Street,_Kampala.jpg *License*: Creative Commons Attribution-Sharealike 2.5 *Contributors*: Doreen Among, uploaded to Wikitravel by Mulo Emmanuel

Image:Africa9 006.jpg *Source*: http://bibliocm.bibliolabs.com/mwAnon/index.php?title=File:Africa9_006.jpg *License*: Public Domain *Contributors*: Original uploader was Michael Shade at en.wikipedia

Image:BahaiTempleKampala.JPG *Source*: http://bibliocm.bibliolabs.com/mwAnon/index.php?title=File:BahaiTempleKampala.JPG *License*: Public Domain *Contributors*: User:NicholasJB

File:Kampala Kasubi Tombs.jpg *Source*: http://bibliocm.bibliolabs.com/mwAnon/index.php?title=File:Kampala_Kasubi_Tombs.jpg *License*: Creative Commons Attribution-Sharealike 2.0 *Contributors*: not not phil from SF, CA, US

File:Kampalas Kasubi Tombs (2064308892).jpg *Source*: http://bibliocm.bibliolabs.com/mwAnon/index.php?title=File:Kampalas_Kasubi_Tombs_(2064308892).jpg *License*: Creative Commons Attribution-Sharealike 2.0 *Contributors*: not not phil from SF, CA, US

File:Siteviewlarge-kasubi tombs-he.jpg *Source*: http://bibliocm.bibliolabs.com/mwAnon/index.php?title=File:Siteviewlarge-kasubi_tombs-he.jpg *License*: Creative Commons Attribution-Sharealike 3.0 *Contributors*: user:גלוד

File:Media BUG 20090501 201118 med.jpg *Source*: http://bibliocm.bibliolabs.com/mwAnon/index.php?title=File:Media_BUG_20090501_201118_med.jpg *License*: Attribution *Contributors*: Scott Cedarleaf/CyArk

File:Kasubi tombs plan detailed cyark.jpg *Source*: http://bibliocm.bibliolabs.com/mwAnon/index.php?title=File:Kasubi_tombs_plan_detailed_cyark.jpg *License*: Attribution *Contributors*: CyArk

Image:commons-logo.svg *Source*: http://bibliocm.bibliolabs.com/mwAnon/index.php?title=File:Commons-logo.svg *License*: logo *Contributors*: User:3247, User:Grunt

File:Mengo mosque.jpg *Source*: http://bibliocm.bibliolabs.com/mwAnon/index.php?title=File:Mengo_mosque.jpg *License*: Creative Commons Attribution 2.0 *Contributors*: Fredrick Onyango from Nairobi, Kenya

Image:Flag of Uganda.svg *Source*: http://bibliocm.bibliolabs.com/mwAnon/index.php?title=File:Flag_of_Uganda.svg *License*: Public Domain *Contributors*: User:Nightstallion

CPSIA information can be obtained at www.ICGtesting.com
Printed in the USA
BVOW01s1803231214

380654BV00005B/77/P